GOOD HABITS

GOOD HABITS

SELF-IMPROVEMENT
FOR THE 1990s

Vincent Ryan Ruggiero

Westminster/John Knox Press
Louisville, Kentucky

Book design by Gene Harris

First edition

Published by Westminster/John Knox Press
Louisville, Kentucky

PRINTED IN THE UNITED STATES OF AMERICA

9   8   7   6   5   4   3   2   1

Library of Congress Cataloging-in-Publication Data

Ruggiero, Vincent Ryan.
   Good habits : self-improvement for the 1990s / Vincent Ryan Ruggiero. — 1st ed.
        p.   cm.
   ISBN 0-664-25198-6
   1. Habit.   2. Self-actualization (Psychology)   3. Conduct of life.
4. Habit breaking.   5. Habit breaking—Religious aspects—
Christianity.   I. Title.
BF335.R83   1991
158—dc20   91-17580

In loving memory of my father,

Vincent V. Ruggiero

Contents

Preface

Millions of people have become disenchanted with the ME-ism that has dominated the last several decades and lingers yet today. ME-ism preaches indulging your desires, doing your own thing in your own way, asserting yourself, and "taking care of number one." It promises success, personal happiness, and freedom from neurosis. Unfortunately, the promise is empty.

During the reign of ME-ism, we have witnessed increasing tolerance of mediocrity and scorn of craftsmanship, growing disregard and even contempt for the sensibilities of others, and erosion of respect for neighbor, family, and country. Worse, we have seen the assassination of three of our leaders, the attempted assassination of several others, and a rise in the incidence of both white-collar and street crime.

We are challenged by a formidable array of social problems, including drug addiction, illiteracy, rape, hate crimes, satanism, spouse abuse, and child molestation. A quarter of our teenagers drop out of school due to pregnancy or loss of interest in learning. Many are lost to drugs, alcohol, or suicide.

At least two lessons can be drawn from these depressing realities: First, a safe and sane world is not possible without respect for the needs and rights of others; second, excellence at work and in our personal lives is never achieved by mere wishing or pretending, but only by effort. Proclaiming ourselves wonderful no more makes us so than chanting "We're number one!" confers athletic success.

A New Perspective

This society desperately needs a different view of self-improvement from the one that has reigned since the 1960s. It needs a no-nonsense back-to-basics perspective that puts competency before self-confidence and replaces self-adulation with self-mastery.

The idea that a ready-made beautiful self resides within everyone is a dangerous fantasy. As Christianity has perennially reminded the world, the self is neither depraved nor inherently good. Rather, it is *deprived*, and so it has the potential for both evil and good, foolishness and wisdom. The choices we make determine which will prevail.

Good Habits reflects this view. It asserts that genuine self-improvement depends not on catch phrases but on practical advice for identifying our imperfections and faults and directing our energies to overcome them. It is based on two facts that are well documented in research and observable in everyday life:

1. Habit is the dominant force operating in our lives, a force so powerful that the ancients called it a "second nature." The degree of success we achieve in our careers and in our personal lives is less influenced by fixed personality traits than by our patterns of thinking, feeling, and doing.

2. Bad habits can be changed. However objectionable they may be, and however long we have tolerated them, we can replace them with good habits if we care enough to invest the effort.

Good Habits explains the role habits play in everyday life, provides a strategy to use in developing your good habits, and identifies more than a hundred specific habits that underlie the most desirable qualities and goals: individuality, efficiency, creativity, sound reasoning, effective communication, moral character, craftsmanship, good relations with others, satisfaction in life, and spirituality.

Deep within every person is a yearning to do something meaningful with his or her life. If the only way to fulfill that yearning were to make a momentous contribution, few of us could ever be fulfilled. Circumstances seldom afford us the chance to be an Albert Einstein, a Winston Churchill, or a Mother Teresa. Yet there is another way to fulfill our yearning, a way no less profound for being more modest. That way is to change the world *within* us. This book can help you reach that goal.

Each is given a bag of tools,

A shapeless mass,

A book of rules;

And each must make,

Ere life is flown,

A stumbling-block

Or a stepping-stone.

R. L. Sharpe

GOOD HABITS

PART ONE

Why Develop Good Habits?

1

The Role of Habit in Everyday Life

"Good morning," I said to the service station attendant. Receiving no acknowledgment, I said, "Fill it up, please, and check the oil."

He put the nozzle into the tank, opened the hood, checked the oil, and mumbled "Oil's OK." Then he finished pumping the gas, took my money, and walked into the office. As I followed him in to get my change, I noticed that he had left the car's hood up. He thrust the change at me and stood glaring.

I asked, "Are you finished under the hood?"

"Yeah." The tone suggested a challenge more than a response.

"Well, aren't you going to shut it?"

"Do you want me to lick your boots, too?"

I'd done business at that station for several years and knew the owner would want to be informed of the incident, so I phoned and told her. She was not surprised. "Though he's only worked here a week," she said, "he's managed to insult several customers. I've spoken to him about it, but it hasn't done any good. I'll probably have to fire him."

A week later he was gone. The bad habit of being uncooperative and surly had cost him his job.

Bad habits frustrate ambitions and cause disappointment and pain. They stifle careers and destroy personal relationships, often leaving people more bitter but little wiser. More important, they often alienate people from God.

Whenever one of Sheldon's proposals is rejected at work he crumples it up, throws it in the trash, and for days rants to his family and friends about the stupidity of his supervisor, the jealousy of his colleagues, the hypocrisy of "the system," and his certainty that he is the victim of prejudice.

Sarah has a creative mind. She regularly conceives new ideas for profitable business ventures and invests considerable enthusiasm and effort in each—for a brief time. But her energy quickly dissipates, and, despite her good intentions and constant daydreaming about success and celebrity, she is seldom able to find the time to finish a project.

Always ready with an instant judgment of problems and issues, Malcolm often has an answer before the question is clarified, especially where old prejudices are involved. Others see him as opinionated and biased, but he prides himself on the constancy of his views in a world of change. He is fond of lamenting that people lack conviction today.

Whenever someone Gina knows acquires something, enjoys some achievement, or gains special recognition, she becomes envious and asks herself, "Why does that person get so much? Is she more worthy than I am? Don't I always try to do the right thing, follow God's teachings, and live a good life?" These episodes frequently leave her feeling vaguely resentful toward God.

Minor changes in behavior would benefit these people greatly. If the service station attendant would just greet customers with a smile, a cheerful word, and a willingness to serve, they'd be satisfied and his job would be more secure. If Sheldon were to resist the temptation to save face, he could profit from his mistakes and increase his chances of success. If Sarah would discipline herself to complete one project before turning to another, her achievements would multiply. If Malcolm would merely open his mind to other views, he would gain people's respect. If Gina would resist the urge to envy and self-pity, she could grow closer to God.

Why do so few people make these small changes? Partly because they find it unpleasant to examine themselves critically and acknowledge the need for change. (It is, after all, more comfortable to justify our behavior than to improve it.) Also, because they have accepted the erroneous yet common notion that qualities such as imaginativeness, logical thinking, efficiency, craftsmanship, moral character, and spirituality cannot be achieved but depend on some inborn talent. Finally, because self-improvement literature has tended to ignore the role good habits play in personal development.

Why Habit Has Been Ignored

Since this century has witnessed an explosion of psychological research, we might well expect pioneering psychologists like Sigmund Freud and B. F. Skinner to have emphasized the formation of good habits. That they did not do so is explainable by their rejection of the Judeo-Christian view of humanity.

Freudians were absorbed with the unconscious mind and its drives, so they slighted such conscious mental processes as creative and critical thinking. Behaviorists, convinced that human beings operate no differently from animals, constructed their theories of human behavior on studies of rats and dogs and pigeons. Both groups rejected the traditional idea that human beings have free will and can choose their thoughts and actions. Consequently, though they acknowledged physical habits, they dismissed mental and spiritual habits as either unimportant or nonexistent. (Not surprisingly, given his view of humans, Skinner even rejected the idea that human beings have any special dignity.)

In the 1960s and 1970s a number of "humanistic" psychologists, notably Abraham Maslow and Carl Rogers, led a reaction against the excesses of Freudianism and behaviorism. That reaction, known as the Human Potential Movement, asserted that there is more to men and women than the merely physical, a higher potential that must be actualized if they are to enjoy fulfillment.

Though in some ways valuable, particularly in its celebration of intuition and creativity, the Human Potential message rested upon three false ideas: that the essential self within each of us is unaffected by the outside world, that feelings are a more genuine expression of the self than thoughts, and that emotional health demands unqualified acceptance of ourselves. Most self-improvement books have leaned heavily on these ideas and so have exalted the self and denied the role of habit.

The Errors Examined

However soothing it may be to believe that the external world does not touch us, in reality it affects us profoundly, for good or for ill. Loving care and guidance in childhood provide a foundation for achievement and happiness. Exploitation and neglect, on the other hand, can create lasting emotional scars. Our sense of right and wrong, our ability or inability to accept responsibility for our actions, and our degree of respect for the rights of others are rooted in the experiences of childhood.

The lessons of the last several decades have made

clear that excellence does not flourish well in every social climate; acceptance of mediocrity breeds mediocrity. Abandoning education standards undermines basic skills, and neglecting reasoning produces students who cannot solve problems or make decisions. And the philosophy of "That's the way I am, don't expect me to change" destroys the very possibility of self-improvement.

Even a casual glance at the daily news is enough to shatter the illusion that feelings are more trustworthy than thoughts. Most warped, self-destructive, and vicious individuals trust their feelings—and are deceived by them. Terrorists *feel* justified in victimizing innocent people, drug and alcohol abusers *feel* in control of their behavior, emaciated anorexics *feel* grossly overweight, would-be teenage suicides *feel* life isn't worth living, rapists *feel* their victims want or deserve to be assaulted, and legions of prison inmates guilty of the most heinous crimes *feel* unjustly convicted.

Far from being more trustworthy than thoughts, feelings are often capricious, reflecting irrational impulse or self-serving fantasy rather than reality. Advertisers have always known this. That is why they design their appeals to make us feel instead of think—to crave the car; to identify the perfume with sexual fulfillment, the beer with camaraderie, the toothpaste with social acceptance. The moment they allow us to think, the spell will be broken and we may recognize the superficiality of their appeals.

Basing self-improvement on feelings invites self-deception. Feeling creative or proficient or wise or moral is not the same as *being* so, which depends on the quality of our responses to the problems and challenges of life. Nor is the quality of those responses governed by good intentions. It is governed by habits.

The third false idea promulgated by humanistic psychology, that emotional health demands unqualified acceptance of self, has proved the most pernicious, for it has provided the foundation of the self-esteem movement. This movement has quickly come to dominate not only psychological theory but educational theory as well. It has even had an impact on contemporary religion. To get an idea of the extent of that impact, consider these quotations from one of the many proponents of self-esteem in religion, Robert H. Schuller: "A person is in hell when he has lost his self-esteem." "Self-esteem . . . is the greatest single need facing the human race today." "The 'will to self-love' is the deepest of all human desires." "The core of original sin then is . . . an innate inability to adequately value ourselves." "The core of sin is a lack of self-esteem."[1]

Does rejecting the popular notion of self-esteem mean rejecting self-worth and human dignity entirely? Not at all. It merely means rejecting the extreme view that self-acceptance must be *unqualified*. Self-loathing is destructive, but self-love can be, too. The ancient myth of Narcissus is a reminder of the danger of excessive preoccupation with self. Jesus admonished us, "Whoever exalts himself shall be humbled." Our age needs a more balanced view of self-esteem, one which emphasizes seeing ourselves honestly, objectively, acknowledging both positive and negative qualities, and building good habits.

Important Facts About Habit

Part of our knowledge of habit is the result of research in our own time. But much has been known for centuries, even millennia. A habit is a pattern of thinking, feeling, or acting. It develops through repetition and in time can become almost automatic, "second nature." The feeling of familiarity created by a habit makes any other response seem strange and inappropriate.

Good habits guide our growth in faith, hope, and charity and our practice of such ideals as justice, kindness, fairness, compassion, and perseverance. Thus they enable us to develop our talents, become more conscientious citizens, workers, spouses, parents, and friends, and deepen our spiritual lives. Bad habits, on the other hand, frustrate our development.

Here are additional important facts about habit:

We have habits of mind as well as physical habits. Contrary to popular belief, habits are not limited to physical activities like typing, driving a car, and dribbling a basketball. There are mental and emotional habits, too. Creativity, logical thinking, and moral living are habits. In fact, the work of many researchers, notably Yale's Robert Sternberg, suggests that intelligence itself is best understood as a complex set of habits.

The teaching of critical and creative thinking, for example, aims at cultivating such habits as postponing judgment, asking probing questions, producing a broad assortment of answers, evaluating sources, and looking for errors in logic. When students develop these and related habits, their responses to problems and issues are both more ingenious and more reasonable.

Habits are acquired rather than inherited. The heredity vs. environment debate is not likely to be settled in the near future. But this much can be said with certainty: Though heredity may influence behavior, it does not determine it. For example, a person with a rapid metabolic rate (a "hyper" person) will have more difficulty learning to be patient than someone with a slow metabolic rate. Yet if the former is brought up in a family in which patience is demonstrated and valued, that person is likely to develop that habit despite his or her metabolism.

Consciously or unconsciously, we are likely to imitate many of our parents' or older siblings' habits. In time we may walk the way they do, adopt the same speech patterns, and even think their thoughts about politics and religion and everyday life. The imitation can be unhealthy, as when an abused child unconsciously follows a parent's example and becomes a child abuser.

When it is positive, however, the family's influence can be a powerful shaper of good habits.

Throughout her illustrious career, actress Helen Hayes was guided by her mother's distinction between achievement and success: "Achievement is the knowledge that you have studied and worked hard and done the best that is in you. Success is being praised by others, and that's nice too, but not as important or as satisfying. Always aim for achievement and forget about success."

Texas industrialist H. Ross Perot was profoundly affected by his mother's habit of charity. One day during the Depression, he discovered why so many beggars came to their door—one beggar had made a mark on the curb to indicate to others that Mrs. Perot was generous. Young Ross suggested she wash the mark off. "No," she responded, "they're good people like us, just down on their luck." Following her example, Perot has given over $100 million to charity.

Our habits tend to reflect the values of our culture. Not long ago I visited Singapore as an education consultant. When I left the United States, newspapers and magazines were filled with stories of various social crises (many of them still with us). Many young people were dropping out of school, victims of apathy, teenage parenthood, or substance abuse. And many of those who stayed graduated illiterate, culturally or completely, or without the thinking and communicating skills necessary to function in well-paying jobs.

The quality of goods and services produced in this country had declined, apparently because many workers lacked a commitment to competency, let alone excellence. Ethical crises were multiplying in government, business, and the professions. Violent crime was making many communities hazardous places to live. Vandalism of cemeteries and synagogues, sometimes involving satanist rituals, was not uncommon. And racial unrest had broken out again on college campuses and some city streets.

Singapore presented a very different reality. I visited a number of schools, some public and some Christian. The principals would take me, unannounced, to classrooms, and as we entered each room, the students would rise to attention and say in unison, "Good morning, principal. Good morning, sir." Then they would return to work, usually in groups. Their enthusiasm for their projects was a joy to observe, their contributions to class discussion spirited.

I met with many students individually and in small groups and found them without exception to be attentive and respectful. To be sure, some were shy about talking to a foreigner. But there was not a trace of apathy or surliness, problems that are still epidemic in many U.S. schools.

People can walk Singapore's streets at 2 A.M. without fear of being robbed or molested. And though Asian drug production is not far from Singapore's borders, the country has no serious drug problem. (One reason, I am sure, is suggested by the sign found on every post at the national airport: WARNING! THE PENALTY FOR DEALING DRUGS IN SINGAPORE IS DEATH.)

The same attitude of respect for other people and for authority I observed in the schools was also evident elsewhere. While waiting to cross a crowded street in downtown Singapore, I noticed that not one of the hundreds of people in or near the intersection jaywalked. Everyone waited patiently for the light to change. Curious, I asked why.

"A few years ago," my host explained, "when jay-walking was outlawed, the police handed out a few tickets and published the offenders' pictures in the newspapers. People don't jaywalk anymore because having their photo in the newspaper for a criminal offense would bring shame on their families."

I was impressed not only by Singaporeans' respect for one another but also by their graciousness to visitors, their dedication to achievement, and their lively wit and intelligence. How do they get such admirable qualities? Are their genes superior to those of Americans? Hardly. Their culture values these qualities and makes an effort to build good habits in its children. The credit goes not to nature but to nurture.

Unless we are vigilant, bad habits are likely to displace good ones. It is not easy to maintain good habits in any culture. As the ancient Roman poet Ovid observed, "Ill habits gather by unseen degrees/ As brooks make rivers, rivers run to seas." Lying, for example, leads to covering up the lie, which leads to deceiving ourselves and believing the lie, which in turn leads to projecting our dishonesty on others and doubting their veracity.

Maintaining good habits is especially difficult today in our culture. Since habit has been ignored for many years, many people are unaware of its force in their lives. More important, popular culture often thwarts the formation of good habits. By using slogans, celebrity testimonials, and appeals that play on people's desires for acceptance and love, advertising encourages people to be gullible and impulsive. The format for commercial television, with its frequent interruptions for clusters of ads, retards viewers' attention span. TV dramas promote a simplistic view of complex issues and a stereotyped view of people. Sensational auto chases, explosions, game-show glitter, and MTV's flashing lights and throbbing sounds create a need for excitement that hinders reflection, which is essential for self-improvement.

Admittedly, popular culture has a positive side. But its negative influences are unrelenting, as are its celebration of mediocrity and its message that fun is more fulfilling than work, self-gratification more fulfilling than self-control, and emotion more trustworthy than reason. Given such a cultural climate, good habits cannot be maintained without continuing effort.

Once we form a bad habit, we're likely to keep it. Suzanne was brought up to believe that an employee should give her employer a day's work for a day's pay. But now that she is working in an office from which the boss is frequently absent, she has started spending considerable time reading magazines and writing personal letters during working hours.

She feels uneasy violating her own principles, but she hasn't tried to break the bad habit. Instead, she has persuaded herself that there is nothing really wrong with what she's doing because it's a common practice, her boss really doesn't assign her enough work to keep her busy, and she's not being paid what she's worth.

Suzanne's line of thought is called rationalizing. It's a common game of pretense people play so they can continue doing things they know can't really be justified. Rationalizing can be used to justify stealing towels from hotels, padding expense accounts, driving while intoxicated, beating a spouse or child, even murder. If people learn to play the game long enough, they may really believe the lies.

One reason the temptation to rationalize is so strong is that breaking a habit, particularly an ingrained one, can be difficult and unpleasant. Consider the habit of saying "he don't" instead of the correct form, "he doesn't." If we are used to saying "he don't," familiarity makes it sound right to us. Conversely, "he doesn't" sounds fussy. To change, we have to be more alert than we want to be, and to suffer through endless occasions of having "he don'ts" slip out when we least expect them, each one a reminder of our failure. It's soothing to think, "It's no big deal to say 'he don't'—after all, it's the idea that counts, not the words."

Habits shape our identity. I was writing something on the blackboard before class. Several undergraduates were talking among themselves, waiting for class to begin. Though I wasn't eavesdropping, I couldn't help hearing their conversation. They were trading jokes about Biafrans. Yes, unbelievable as it may sound, they were finding humor in the condition of those helpless skeletal figures with distended bellies and beseeching eyes, fellow human beings starving to death.

I had encountered insensitivity and callousness before—guffawing at movie scenes of slaughter, snickering during serious discussions of rape, squeals of what seemed to be pleasure over photos of a household pet hit by a car. Still, I was unprepared for jokes about starvation. I turned around and studied the students' faces. Not one seemed aware of the obscenity of their conversation.

Perhaps I should have said something, but I didn't. It was easy to predict the reaction I would get: "Lighten up, prof, we're only having some fun. We don't mean any harm."

Wishes and good intentions aside, what we think and say and do is what we are. If we base our judgments on evidence, we are rational; if on preconceptions, irrational. If we tell the truth, we are truthful; if we lie, we are liars. If we live by the same standards we demand of others, we are honest people; if not, we are hypocrites. And if we laugh at human suffering, we are less than fully human.

No one is perfectly consistent, let alone perfect. A rational person may occasionally become irrational, just as a liar may tell the truth now and again. Our measure as people is not the isolated instance but the pattern of our behavior, what we characteristically think and say and do. And these things are intimately bound up with our habits.

Though it is common to speak of people possessing habits, it is important to recognize the other side of that truth. *Habits possess people!*

Good habits are the best mechanism for coping with stress and complexity. Much has been written about coping with the stress and complexity of everyday life. Prescriptions run the gamut from primal screaming to sitting like a pretzel and chanting "Ohmmm." In fact, the only approach that has lacked a champion is the eminently sensible approach of developing good habits.

The merchandise had to be shipped by UPS from a warehouse in another state. Delivery, the clerk said, would take from three to five days. My speaking schedule takes me away from home for days at a time. Wanting the package to arrive when I was there, I wrote these instructions on the store's order form: *Please arrange for delivery between 10/16 and 10/18—customer will be traveling before then.*

When the sixteenth and the seventeenth came and passed with no delivery, I called the store and spoke to the woman in charge of special orders. "I've waited for two days," I explained. "I just want to be sure that everything is OK and the order will be here soon."

"Oh, I didn't place the order yet. Since you were traveling, I figured I'd play it safe and place it after you were home."

"But the order said I wanted delivery between the sixteenth and the eighteenth. I had a reason for specifying that: I'll be leaving again on the nineteenth for another trip."

"Well, I was just trying to be helpful."

However pure her intentions may have been, following careless assumptions instead of explicit directions was a mistake. If she allows that mistake to become a habit—and a single act can be the foundation of a habit—her job will surely be in jeopardy.

A young college student I know lost a very desirable part-time job in just that way. Jimmy was answering the telephone in the advertising department of a large metropolitan newspaper at $10 an hour. His supervisor told him exactly what to say and how to say it.

Jimmy assumed the instructions were merely a rough guideline and that creativity would be appreciated. When the supervisor overheard him violating the instructions, he warned him. Jimmy then assumed the warning was merely "for the record," that the supervisor really intended to give him the latitude he wanted. When the supervisor overheard him again, Jimmy's desirable job came to an abrupt end.

Good habits could have spared both Jimmy and the woman who processed my order the stress they experienced. And good habits can do the same for you. For example, if you are an efficient person who meets life imaginatively, reasons soundly, and communicates clearly, you will avoid many of the problems that plague other people. Similarly, if you behave ethically, take pride in your work, and maintain good relations with others, your life will be less complicated by friction, frustration, and negative emotions.

Moreover, on those occasions when stress occurs, as it inevitably does from time to time in even the best-regulated lives, good habits can help you deal with it more effectively. The habits associated with wisdom and satisfaction in life, for instance, will enable you to confront challenges calmly and with equanimity.

Good habits can bring us closer to God. In the parable of the sower, Jesus describes how some seeds fell by the road and were eaten by birds, some fell in rocky places and were scorched by the sun, some fell among thorns and were choked off, and some fell upon good ground and thrived. The seeds, Jesus then explains, represent God's word sown in the human heart; what happens to those seeds depends on how people receive them. If people lack understanding, "the evil one comes and snatches [the word] away." If they receive the word joyfully but lack a "firm root" in themselves, they will forsake it in difficult times. And if they allow it to be choked off by the "worry of the world" and "the deceitfulness of riches," it will be unfruitful (Matt. 13:3–8, 18–22).

Good habits can help us receive God's word in the way God wishes, hearing and understanding it and making it bear fruit. They cultivate in us a spirit of understanding, help us form a right perspective on both the spiritual and the secular, and foster the discipline to turn intentions into deeds and live what we believe.

We have the power to choose the habits we want. The neglect of habit formation in our culture and the denial of people's capacity for self-mastery have had a tragic effect on millions of lives. Yet a single fact offers powerful reason for optimism: Whether we keep our habits or change them is a matter of choice. There is no need for us to be victimized by biology or by past experiences. With God's help, we can conquer bad habits and form good ones whenever we wish. Everyday life is filled with dramatic examples of this truth. Alcoholics and drug addicts have overcome their enslavement, slothful people have become industrious, thieves have reformed, violent people have curbed their emotions, selfish people have transcended their egos, sinners have become saints.

Even if your habits of thinking and acting have their roots in victimization by tragic circumstance, you can change them. You may, for example, have been subjected to poverty and deprivation in a ghetto, or abused by your parents, or merely raised permissively and indulgently. Whatever the case, you can assert control over your habits and transform them.

Chris grew up in the shadow of his older brother, Tom. Tom was always saying clever, amusing things. Their parents were obviously delighted with Tom. Partly out of admiration and partly out of envy, Chris began imitating his brother. Competing with Tom for attention was not easy. To get his parents' attention—indeed, to get a word in edgewise—he had to express thoughts as soon as they popped into his mind, without sorting them out for sense or appropriateness.

The habit of blurting out thoughts changed Chris dramatically. His answers in class were often ludicrous, so teachers came to view him as unintelligent. And his friends, stung by what they regarded as his insensitivity and sarcasm, deserted him one by one. For many years Chris persuaded himself that people just didn't have his refined sense of humor.

Then, in a moment of introspection in his mid-thirties, he realized what the problem was and why it had developed. "I can't change the fact that my parents favored Tom or that I made myself into a pathetic imitation of him to earn their love," he admitted, "but I can break the bad habits I developed." He resolved to delay expressing his thoughts until he weighed them first and determined that they made sense and would not hurt others' feelings. Each time he reacted mindlessly, he redoubled his efforts. In time, he conquered the old habit and recovered friendships.

Like Chris, you can overcome your bad habits. If you reject constructive criticism, you can learn to accept it graciously. If you ignore unpleasant realities, you can learn to face them courageously. If you give up when frustrated or confused, you can become persevering. If you leap to conclusions without weighing evidence, you can learn to be reflective. If you indulge in rationalizing and face-saving to avoid acknowledging your faults, you can learn to be honest with yourself and others. And if material goals have displaced spiritual ones and made you value *having* more than *being* and *doing*, you can restore your sense of priorities.

The power to change your habits is among the most wonderful of God's gifts. Animals are captive to their instincts and so must be what they are. Unlike them, you can decide the kind of person you ought and want to be and set about becoming that person.

2

A Strategy
for Developing
Good Habits

The day after France surrendered to Nazi Germany, Pastor André Trocmé urged his parishioners to fight the invaders with "the weapons of the spirit." From that moment until the end of the war, the five thousand people of his village of Le Chambon responded heroically, risking their own lives to save the lives of the Jews they came in contact with, five thousand in all. Despite the history of anti-Semitism throughout Europe and the collaborationist mood of the country, not a single person betrayed the heroic effort.

Felipe Garza, a poor fifteen-year-old from Patterson, California, had a crush on Donna Ashlock, fourteen. When he learned that she was suffering from an enlarged heart and was not expected to survive for longer than two months, he told his mother, "If I die, give my heart to my girlfriend." Shortly thereafter, a blood vessel ruptured in his brain, killing him, and Donna received his gift of life.

Stories like these touch us deeply. They provide dramatic proof that there are higher levels of humanness than those acknowledged by our egocentric, materialistic age. And they challenge us to raise our aspirations and strive to attain those levels. Thus they make an excellent springboard for self-improvement.

Be Inspired by the Good Habits of Others

The first step to take in developing your own good habits is to be inspired by those of others. Television news would seem an obvious place to look for such inspiration. Unfortunately, it is not easy to find there. George Washington University's Media Analysis Project evaluated 85,000 words in hundreds of broadcasts over 100 days and found only 47 positive statements. The conclusion: "Bad news is reported on TV twenty times more than good news."

So look not just at TV news but in newspapers and magazines. More importantly, look around your own community. Though they may not receive banner headlines, stories like these are happening every day.

Jeff Street of Chandler, Arizona, sent a former employer a $326 check, explaining that as a sixteen-year-old he had stolen $40 from a cash register and wanted to reimburse the employer, with interest, for his "inexcusable" act.

Trainman John Kohl of Northumberland, Pennsylvania, realized that his Conrail train could not stop in time to miss a two-year-old girl who had crawled out on the tracks. So he crawled out onto the cowcatcher, leaned forward precariously, and swatted the girl to safety.

For the past twenty-four years, between Thanksgiving and Christmas, Michael Greenberg, a retired advertising executive, has given out gloves to the down-and-out men and women in New York City's Bowery. In doing so, he honors the memory and follows the example of his father, a Brooklyn baker who during the

Depression would slip a cake or a sandwich into customers' bags without their knowing. (His father's philosophy: "Don't deprive yourself of the joy of giving.")

Over the years Hector and Susan Badeau have adopted seventeen children, all of them "special needs" cases—for example, learning-disabled, malnourished, or suffering from a crippling disease.

One hundred fourteen cartoonists, including Charles Schulz *(Peanuts)*, Garry Trudeau *(Doonesbury)*, and Milton Caniff *(Steve Canyon)* devoted their Thanksgiving Day cartoons to the subject of hunger and donated their artwork for advertisements soliciting donations for world hunger relief.

Antoinette Ellis, a Philadelphia sixteen-year-old and one of fifteen children, spends all her spare time helping people. She runs errands for senior citizens, plays bingo with them, and helps with neighborhood cleanup projects.

Keep a file of such uplifting stories and look back on them from time to time. Ask yourself what specific habits they reveal and how you can best develop those habits yourself.

Take an Honest Look at Yourself

The second step in developing good habits is to take a look at yourself. "Look in the mirror, acknowledge what you see there, and resolve to change what needs changing." That's the advice you would receive at the outset of a weight-loss or body-building program. The same sensible advice applies to the development of good mental, emotional, and spiritual habits.

There are differences, of course. For one thing, there are no mirrors you can use to check the patterns of your thoughts, feelings, and actions. For another, you have undoubtedly built up an intricate network of defenses to justify your bad habits, and these will make it difficult for you to assess your behavior accurately.

Such defenses, though unfortunate, are perfectly normal. We all want to think well of ourselves, so we tend to place the best interpretation on what we think and feel and do, even if that interpretation distorts reality.

For years I asked students in my college classes in critical thinking, "Who was the person you most disliked as a teenager? Why did you dislike that person?" Though I didn't say so in advance, my main purpose in asking was to help them recognize how easily perception can be distorted. When I examined their written responses, which were usually rich in angry detail, I found almost none of the students ever blamed themselves for disliking people, even when it seemed evident that some failing of their own, such as pettiness or jealousy, was at least partly responsible for their animosity.

Someone would write, for example, "I disliked Mary because she was the most popular girl in school. All the boys flocked around her and the teachers held her up for admiration. She thought she was better than the rest of us. She disgusted me!" Now it is possible that the popular girl was haughty and vain, but equally possible that the writer was simply envious of her.

Why is such distortion of reality so common? Because it's easier to point the finger of criticism at others than at ourselves. As a test, try this experiment: Extend your arm and point your index finger away from you. Now turn your arm around and point it toward yourself. It's more difficult the second way, isn't it? That difficulty exists mentally and spiritually as well as physically.

Joseph Mengele was one of the most barbarous individuals in history, having designed and implemented devilish experiments that tortured and murdered tens of thousands of innocent inmates of Nazi concentration

camps. But did he consider himself a barbarian? Surely
not. Most likely he focused on the positive aspects of his
life—born to a wealthy and respected Bavarian family,
well educated (holding both Ph.D. and M.D. degrees),
loyal to his political party and beliefs—and explained
away the darker realities.

It's not hard to imagine Mengele thinking, as many
Nazis did, Ignorant people will not understand, but I am
serving science and one day my name will be honored.

Less extreme cases reveal the same kind of self-deception. I know a woman, I'll call her Ann, who is lazy and
irresponsible. She treats her personal and household belongings carelessly, arrives late for appointments, and
ignores overdue notices from her creditors. In addition,
she neglects her duties as a parent, refusing to teach her
children table manners, personal hygiene, or respect for
other people.

Yet Ann would be flabbergasted if anyone accused her
of being lazy and irresponsible. Her treatment of her
belongings she explains by referring to the biblical in-
junction not to place too much value on material things.
When friends complain about her tardiness, she accuses
them of having hang-ups; when creditors grow impatient, she charges them with being greedy and heartless.
And she argues that her approach to parenting is more
enlightened than the traditional approach. "Children,"
she argues, "learn the lessons of life better through experience than through parental preaching."

Ann's self-justifications may spare her from feeling
guilty (temporarily, at least), but they also prevent her
from experiencing the dissatisfaction that genuine self-
improvement depends upon.

There is no point in improving what doesn't need
improving. If you look in the mirror and make believe
you see a taut, athletic body, you surely won't be motivated to begin a diet or an exercise program. Similarly,
pretending to have no bad habits leads to compla-

cency rather than action. Only when you are disturbed by what you see will you be moved to change it. (That's why the popular view of self-esteem, unqualified acceptance of self, hinders rather than aids self-improvement.)

The point of seeing yourself critically, of course, is not to blame yourself (or your parents) but merely to identify habits that need changing. Blaming is a pointless, negative activity. Identifying bad habits is part of the process that makes you feel *justifiably* good about yourself.

The best way to see yourself from a fresh perspective is to look at yourself through other people's eyes. Take a pencil and paper and write down all the criticisms other people have expressed about you in recent months. Keep the list handy for the next few days and add to it whenever you remember another criticism.

Be especially careful not to screen out any criticisms, even ones you are convinced are unfair. Those may prove to be the most accurate. Admit that you, like other people, become most defensive when what is said about you is true. Then, when you recall a particular criticism and find yourself becoming upset and muttering, "That's wrong—she just doesn't understand," instead of rejecting the criticism, write it in CAPITAL LETTERS.

If you have difficulty using this approach, remind yourself that at this stage you are merely noting other people's criticisms, not accepting them. There will be ample opportunity later to decide that a particular criticism is unfounded. By postponing that decision, you increase the likelihood that you will make it rationally.

After you have compiled a thorough list, review what you have written and underline any criticisms that have been made by more than one person or in more than one situation. Those will be most deserving of your attention.

Monitor Your Behavior

The next step in developing good habits is to watch for the appearance of the traits included on your list. Sometimes bad habits (and good ones) occur in clusters, one triggering and reinforcing another. A young man I know, for example, is the youngest of four highly competitive brothers. To bolster his own confidence, Marvin developed the habit of predicting how well he would do before competing with one of his brothers. "You're in for it today," he would say. "I'm going to whip you soundly."

Whenever he fell behind in a competition, he would envision how acute his embarrassment would be if he lost. Desperate to win, he became a poor sport, making derogatory comments about his opponent's game, doings things to distract him, even cheating on the score. And whenever he lost, he sought to save face by accusing his brother of cheating or by feigning an injury. ("If I hadn't turned my ankle early on, the outcome would have been different.") His brothers usually saw through these transparent excuses and teased him. Marvin's first response to their jibes was pretended outrage, but habit soon made it real.

Rather than acknowledge to himself that his prediction of victory was a bad habit that led to several other bad habits, he persuaded himself to make his predictions even more sweeping and bombastic. In time his brothers refused to play with him at all.

In monitoring your behavior, be sure to look not just for single habits but also for clusters. And in observing your actions, be alert for the feelings and thoughts that immediately precede actions. The more you understand how your undesirable behavior is triggered, the better your chances of overcoming it.

For example, if one of the traits on your list is becoming angry and berating others, try to catch yourself displaying that trait. And whenever you do so, note what you were thinking and feeling just before and just as you got angry. It might be an unspoken sentence—She has no business questioning me; I'm in charge here—or simply a surge of emotion: embarrassment, perhaps, or resentment.

The aim here is to gather all the data you can for later analysis. If you feel uncomfortable monitoring your own behavior, remind yourself that doing so is less an embarrassment than an opportunity. After all, through your formative years you studied a variety of subjects—other people's lives, plants, animals, and the history of numerous academic subjects—but never yourself. Now that you have that chance, make the most of it.

Evaluate Your Findings

The fourth step in developing good habits is evaluation. After you have monitored your behavior for a reasonable time, review your findings and decide to what extent (if any) other people's criticisms of you are accurate. At this point you may be tempted to self-deception. Here are the forms it usually takes and some strategies for dealing with each.

"That never happened." As improbable as it sounds, denial of unpleasant realities is common. Let's say others have complained that when someone disagrees with you, you grow agitated, raise your voice, and interrupt their remarks with hostile challenges. During the monitoring stage, you may behave that way numerous times, yet each time you *misperceive* your actions as spirited discussion rather than offensive behavior. The antidote to such denial is to remind yourself, in both the monitoring and evaluating stages, that face-saving can alter perception, and "That never happened" may merely be a dishonest way of saying "I don't want to acknowledge that."

"I was justified in behaving that way." Sometimes your behavior will be justifiable. Self-deception occurs when you make excuses in an effort to justify what is unjustifiable. This form of self-deception is best dealt with by recalling a situation in which someone else behaved similarly, and you disapproved, and then asking yourself, Shouldn't my behavior be condemned for the same reason?

"It isn't that big a deal." This form of self-deception minimizes the bad habit. For example, you may say to yourself, There are many habits that are more offensive than this one, so I needn't waste time overcoming it. Remind yourself that since small bad habits often lead to big ones, time spent overcoming any bad habit is time well spent.

"Look who's talking!" This reaction shifts attention to the person who criticized you and implies that if he or she isn't perfect, your bad habit somehow doesn't count. Remind yourself that other people's faults have no bearing on your self-improvement. Your emphasis should be on yourself.

Make your judgments about your behavior explicit by writing them down on paper. Be brutally honest and avoid making excuses. Write in this manner:

I tend to be a conformist. I prefer familiar thoughts to unfamiliar ones. Somehow they seem safer to me. In examining my thinking I find a lot of slogans and generalizations that I never really analyzed but just picked up from people around me.

At times I take advantage of others, including friends and family. Worse, I lie to myself about it, saying they deserve the treatment and no one else will look out for me if I don't look out for myself. I'm too quick to justify myself and make excuses for my faults.

My intentions are usually noble, and I can be proud of that. But I sometimes make that virtue a vice. I get so preoccupied by thoughts of making the heroic gesture that I miss dozens of daily opportunities to do good on a more modest scale.

If expressing unpleasant facts about yourself on paper proves difficult, reflect on the following thought when you sit down to write: Your purpose is not to denigrate but to elevate yourself. Any feelings of guilt and self-recrimination you experience now will be transformed into satisfaction and heightened self-respect the moment you begin replacing bad habits with good ones.

Set Goals and Strive to Reach Them

Now you are ready to take the fifth step in developing good habits: Use the knowledge you've gained about yourself to identify the personal qualities you want to develop and to begin acquiring the habits associated with them. The second part of this book discusses ten of the most desirable qualities, identifies the various good habits that underlie them, and suggests ways to develop those good habits in everyday situations.

In working on your good habits, be sure to choose a pace that is comfortable for you. Spend a month or more on a single quality, if you wish, devoting a week or so to each associated habit. Or, if you prefer, set a more ambitious pace, working on two or three qualities simultaneously.

Whatever pace you decide is right for you, remember that old habits aren't easily disposed of. As Mark Twain cautioned, you can't throw a habit out the window; you must coax it downstairs a step at a time. So be both patient and persistent.

To ensure that your good habits become firmly rooted, reinforce your actions with appropriate thoughts and feelings. Here's how you'd proceed in three typical situations.

You are working on EFFICIENCY, specifically on the habit of completing unpleasant tasks first. Begin each day by reminding yourself that you wish to develop this habit because putting unpleasant tasks aside "until later" prolongs uncomfortable feelings unnecessarily. In addition, recall the sense of relief and satisfaction you experience when you complete unpleasant tasks.

You are working on WISDOM, specifically on the habit of acknowledging your ignorance (at least to yourself). Before every encounter with someone you wish to impress—your employer, for example, or a good friend—remind yourself that no one can be expected to know everything and that when conversation turns to something you know little about, the most sensible approach is not to keep talking, pretending knowledge; it is to listen and learn. In addition, recall how at ease you have felt when you've been honest with yourself and others.

You are working on GOOD RELATIONS WITH OTHERS, specifically on the habit of expressing affection and love. Remind yourself that people have no way of knowing how you feel about them unless you express your feelings. And recall how wonderful you feel when people you care about let you know that the sentiments are reciprocated.

Using thoughts and feelings in this way brings an additional benefit: providing encouragement when you need it. No matter how dedicated you may be to improving yourself, there will be times when you tire of the conscious effort required. At these times you will be tempted to revert to old ways and thus undermine the progress you've made. Reminding yourself of your goals and the benefits they represent will help you resist the temptation and continue striving.

Ask God to Bless and Guide Your Efforts

It might seem that if people know what they should do, truly want to do it, and devise a plan for doing it, success is assured. Ironically, that is seldom the case. Some people never get beyond the planning stage. Others start but eventually lose their determination or forget their goal and their reason for pursuing it. In the frantic pace of modern living, it's easy to lose sight of our priorities and neglect all but the most insistent tasks.

The only way to be sure that your commitment to good habits does not become one more good intention you never carry out is to take it to God and ask for His blessing and continued guidance. This is the final and most important step in developing good habits. Here is a prayer to assist you. To keep your attention focused on your goal, repeat the prayer daily.

Heavenly Father, you know how many times I have wanted to improve myself and become what you want me to be. You know, too, how often my intentions have failed to bear fruit; my spirit is ever willing, but my flesh is all too weak. Now I have resolved to express my love for you by overcoming my bad habits and developing good ones. I know this can only be accomplished one small step at a time. Please bless my efforts and give me the strength to persevere.

PART TWO

A Guide to Forming Good Habits

3

Habits
for Individuality

The popular view is that everyone possesses individuality from birth; that it is somehow in our genes and nothing can alter it. According to this view, each of us must be an individual; whatever we do, consciously or otherwise, is an expression of our uniqueness.

This view is unrealistic. It ignores the fact that we are influenced by our experiences. If we were not, learning would be impossible. Our senses are taking in information from the moment of birth. Hearing and touch, in fact, are operating even before birth.

The language our parents speak is the one we learn. The music, art, and literature we are exposed to shape our tastes. The sentiments, preferences, and convictions our parents and teachers share with us—about the world and the people and institutions in it—affect us profoundly. Even as we grow older and become more able to decide for ourselves, the habits and attitudes and values of our culture continue to exert a powerful influence on us, in some cases greater than that of our parents.

Individuality, in the most meaningful sense, is not something we are born with but something to be achieved.

Identify Key Influences in Your Life

The first step in developing individuality is determining what influences have molded you. The most obvious
ones are the home, the school, and the church. But over
the the past thirty or forty years another powerful influence, popular culture, has gained dominance. In many
cases, popular culture challenges and displaces all other
influences.

Which parent had more influence on you, your
mother or your father? And precisely what was that influence, on your thinking and behaving? On your goals
and aspirations in life?

If you had brothers or sisters, what did you most admire about them? What did you consciously imitate in
them? In what ways do you now see you unconsciously
did so? Were aunts, uncles, cousins, and grandparents
also influential? Whom did you admire outside your family, a teacher or clergyman, perhaps, or a close friend?
How did these people help to shape you?

Be sure to consider small influences as well as great,
subtle as well as obvious ones. "Once when I was a little
girl, my grandfather told me that what we read goes
deep inside us and becomes a part of us," a friend told
me recently. "For some reason I've remembered those
words for almost sixty years. To this day I feel guilty
whenever I read trash."

Chances are, the influence of popular culture, though
less obvious than that of home, school, and church, was
at least as strong. If you were a typical TV viewer during
your childhood, by age eighteen you had spent 22,000
hours in front of the TV set, compared to 11,000 in the
classroom. And you saw over three quarters of a million
print and TV advertisements, each selling not only goods
and services but attitudes and values.[2]

How much did radio, TV, popular magazines, books,
and music affect you? In what ways did they challenge

what you learned at home? These are critical questions.
If you are like many people who have grown up in this
culture in the last forty years, you have rejected some of
your parents' values, believing that you were expressing
individuality in so doing, whereas in fact you may have
been succumbing to the influence of popular culture.
Much of what you now regard as your authentic inner
self may merely be a reflection of the popular culture's
influence on you, an influence you have never recognized or acknowledged.

Of course, parental influence is not necessarily positive, nor is popular culture's influence necessarily negative. It is possible that parents, teachers, and religious
leaders offered you misinformed, shallow, even prejudiced views. And the examples they set may have been
less than admirable. On the other hand, their counsel
may have been wiser than you were able to see at the
time. Once you identify the influences in your life, you
will be able to evaluate them.

Good-Habit Builder

List the important influences in your life. Keep this list
handy. Subsequent Good-Habit Builders will refer to it.

Examine Your Beliefs

The term "beliefs" covers a wide range of matters,
from philosophical and religious convictions to views
about parenting and politics and positions on current
controversial issues. You may find the idea of examining
such matters unpleasant. To do so may seem to suggest
either that you are irresponsible or that your parents
and teachers did you a disservice, or both. In reality, it
suggests no such thing.

In this age of mass communication, we are bombarded
with ideas virtually every waking moment. No one has

time to sort out all these ideas and determine their relative worth. Sheer repetition of an idea in the media can fool us. Mistaking familiarity for merit, we may unwisely change our beliefs. By periodically examining our beliefs, we are able to restore the earlier, better ones. Often this means honoring our parents and teachers by reaffirming the wisdom they imparted.

But even if our examination leads us to reject what our parents and teachers taught us, it does them no disservice. On the contrary, it is an act of intellectual humility that says, in effect, "Surely they would never have intentionally misled us. They tried their best to lead us to the truth. Nevertheless, they were human and therefore capable of error. We owe it to them, to ourselves, and most importantly to God to carry on the effort they began—to probe further, overcome error, and deepen our understanding of truth."

This process of examining beliefs will cause you to discard some beliefs, but only when there is good reason to do so. At other times, it will strengthen your commitment to those that are worthy. The following questions will help you identify some of your most important beliefs.

What Are Your Religious Beliefs?

Consider not only whether you are a believer and, if you are, what religious denomination you belong to, but what your views are on fundamental religious questions. For example, decide what you believe about creation. Do you accept the biblical account, the theory of evolution, or some combination of the two, such as, "I believe God created all things through the process called evolution, but infused a soul into the first humans"?

Decide, too, what you believe a human being's relationship with God should be, what God expects of us; whether the Bible is the inerrant word of God; whether Jesus is the Son of God; whether there is an afterlife;

whether sincere believers in other religions can be saved; and in what specific ways your daily life should reflect your religious beliefs.

What Are Your Political Beliefs?

Ask yourself what you believe the purpose of government is, what its proper role is, and what governmental initiatives, if any, overstep that role. Consider all the agencies of government and their responsibilities, including health, defense, education, welfare, and various regulatory functions. Determine what obligations, if any, citizens have toward their country.

What Are Your Beliefs About Marriage and Family Life?

Decide whether you believe marriage is a human or a divine institution, when (if ever) divorce is morally permissible, and what specific obligations married people have to their spouses. Consider what parents owe their children, when and in what ways they should discipline them, and what lessons they should be especially diligent about teaching them. What do you believe are the characteristics of an ideal parent?

Think, too, about the obligations of children to parents. Medical advances continue to lengthen lives, but many older people lack financial means, particularly when the high cost of illness exhausts their resources. In such cases, do you believe children should be financially responsible for their parents? What other obligations, if any, do adult children have to their parents?

What Are Your Beliefs Concerning Important Social Issues?

Many important issues challenge us today. Environmental and animal rights activists argue that forests and animals should enjoy the same rights that people do. Proponents of sex education call for expanded programs in the schools. Many social critics say the depiction of violence on television and in the movies causes actual violence and therefore should be banned. Some people believe that the solution to our educational problems lies in raising teachers' salaries and giving them more control over the curriculum, while others believe fundamental changes must be made in educational philosophy and objectives.

In recent decades traditional morality has been increasingly challenged. Many believe that there is no objective moral code binding on all people. They say the majority decides what is right and wrong, or that each individual decides on the basis of personal preference and desire. The current debates over the morality of suicide and euthanasia reflect these challenges to the traditional view.

Decide what you believe about these and other important social issues. Write down your thoughts, and don't be surprised if the act of writing them down causes you some confusion. Very often what seems clear in our minds proves to be less so when we commit it to paper. Try to overcome confusion by rephrasing your answers until they mirror your thoughts. Then evaluate each of your beliefs as fair-mindedly as you can, setting aside the obvious attachment you have formed for it and asking whether it deserves to be maintained.

Good-Habit Builder

Review the beliefs you listed and try to decide the origin of each. Recall people who exerted a strong influence in your life: parents, teachers, religious leaders, friends. Recall personal experiences, too. If any belief seems unrelated either to these individuals or to these experiences, consider the possibility that you absorbed it unthinkingly from popular culture. (Such beliefs merit careful analysis.)

Examine Your Attitudes and Emotions

Attitudes are often more difficult to identify than beliefs. Whereas beliefs tend to be conscious, attitudes tend to be unconscious. They are generally felt rather than thought. Yet their impact is no less powerful: They predispose the mind to see a person, place, or thing favorably or unfavorably and thus influence beliefs. Thus, if carelessly or irresponsibility formed, attitudes lead us into error and injustice.

One effective way to identify your attitudes is to notice the associations that particular people, places, and things have for you, the ideas they call to mind. Associations may be favorable, neutral, unfavorable, or a combination of all three. The associations you have for "Italians," for example, may be "artistic," "violent," "vivacious," "excitable," or "sinister." Associations usually provide a good indication of your attitudes.

Following are some groups of people, as well as some places and things. To identify your attitude toward each, list the associations that come to mind:

Catholics, Protestants, Jews, agnostics, atheists
Caucasians, African Americans, Hispanics, Asians
Germans, Poles, Russians, Arabs, the Irish
Democrats, Republicans, Socialists, Communists
Doctors, dentists, lawyers, accountants, teachers, televangelists, athletes
The inner city, the South, the Midwest, California, New York City, Texas, New England
Homosexuality, feminism, humanism, capitalism, welfare

Closely related to attitudes are emotions, the positive or negative feelings that we experience and that shape our actions. Attitudes and emotions tend to be mutually reinforcing. If your associations for Jews are favorable, you will be inclined to feel friendly toward them, even at first meeting. If your associations for Arabs are unfavorable, you will probably regard them with suspicion, even hostility. In either case, the emotions you experience will usually strengthen your prior attitudes, especially if you act on these emotions.

The following questions will help you identify your emotions and the attitudes they reflect.

What Do You Fear?

Some people's fears are paralyzing. Acrophobes may grow dizzy and begin to tremble at the mere thought of being in a high place. Agoraphobes will sometimes refuse to leave their homes because of their fear of open or public places. Most people's fears are less dramatic and more manageable than these. They may even be so subtle as to be thought of as something else. For example, we may say "I prefer to keep my ideas to myself" instead of "I am afraid people will find my thoughts shallow and laugh at me."

To discover your fears, identify situations you find unpleasant, and try to avoid, and situations that make you upset even to contemplate. Then ask, Why do I react that way? What about those situations causes me concern?

What Makes You Angry?

Like other emotions, anger is neither inherently good nor inherently bad. We can judge it only by considering when it occurs and how we handle it. It is appropriate to become angry at someone who has insulted us in front of other people, but inappropriate to become angry at a colicky infant. If two people become angry at corruption in government (an appropriate feeling), and one reacted by supporting a reform candidate while the other gave up voting in elections, we would applaud the former but not the latter.

Before you can judge your anger, you must first identify it and examine its effects. To do so, think of as many situations as you can in which you became angry. Recall exactly what you were angry about, what thoughts went through your mind, and what you said and did as a result of your anger.

Whom Do You Respect and Admire?

The people we admire and the things we admire about them can tell us a great deal about our attitudes and values. If we admire mostly wealthy people because of their financial status and material possessions, we will define success in very different terms from someone who admires the Albert Schweitzers and Mother Teresas of the world. If we admire people in positions of power and authority, the "winners" of this world, we may have little sympathy for the underdogs.

Make a list of the people you admire and respect and explain what about them most impresses you. Then consider what your admiration reveals about your attitudes and values.

Good-Habit Builder

Examine each attitude you identified. Decide whether you unconsciously borrowed it from your parents, or someone else, or whether you deliberately cultivated it. Decide, too, whether it is a reasonable, wholesome attitude. (It's natural to want to maintain our attitudes, so you'll have to force yourself to make this judgment impartially.)

Examine each emotion you identified. Is it similar to

that displayed by someone close to you, for example a parent? Decide whether you should be proud or ashamed of it.

Study Your Reactions to People and Ideas

The messenger attached the message pouch to his saddle, mounted his horse, and rode, hour after hour throughout the day. When evening fell, he slept, but then at sunup was on his way again. Three days later, he arrived at the castle, dismounted, sprinted in to the king, then knelt quietly as the king read the message. His face darkening at the bad news, the king cursed and ordered the messenger beheaded.

The ancient practice of executing the bearer of bad tidings seems ludicrous to us (not to mention unfair). But modern people's reaction to bad news may be just as unreasonable. When government employees report corruption or waste to the proper authorities, they are often scorned by their peers and harassed by their superiors. When citizens complain to a school board about a policy or procedure they regard as unfair or harmful to children, they are more likely to be resented than lauded, even if their position is eminently reasonable. As Winston Churchill once remarked, many consider it worse to point out an offense than to commit it.

It's easier, of course, to see the foolishness of other people's reactions than the foolishness of our own. That's why it's important to study our own reactions closely, particularly the habitual, more or less unconscious ones. What we do consciously, thoughtfully, is likely to be an expression of our individuality because we exert control over it. Unconscious reactions, on the other hand, usually control us!

The following questions will help you identify your reactions to people and ideas and gain greater control over those reactions.

What Are Your Interests?

There are no interesting or uninteresting subjects, only interested or disinterested people. It may please us to think that we choose our own interests, but in most cases they are a matter of conditioning. If you were never exposed to classical music or great books or the theater or art while growing up, you probably have little interest in them now.

One way to become more of an individual is to make a conscious effort to broaden your interests. That doesn't mean trying to become interested in everything; it merely means giving yourself opportunities to develop new interests. Start by considering all the things you are now interested in. Then select one or two subjects you *aren't* interested in but are willing to give a chance to prove themselves.

How Do You Approach Problems?

Since problem solving is seldom taught in any systematic way in school, most people perform the activity more or less haphazardly. They may have a characteristic approach, but since they haven't ever really thought it out, they are only vaguely aware of it.

Here's how you can learn about your problem solving. The next time a problem arises at work or in your personal life, be aware of how you deal with it. Perhaps you'll find that an image comes to mind. On the other hand, you might silently focus on a word or statement or raise a question. Observe what you do during each step of the process. Notice whether you follow any special procedure and how you react when you encounter obstacles or dead ends.

At first you may find it uncomfortable or distracting to use your mind in two ways at once—both working on the problem and analyzing what you are doing—but you will soon get used to doing so. As you learn more about your approach to problem solving, consider how you can improve it.

How Do You React to Disagreement?

Think of a recent occasion when someone disagreed strongly with something you said. Was your immediate reaction, Well, I could be wrong; let's explore the issue and see? Chances are, it wasn't. The most common first reaction at such times is to think, How dare he challenge my idea? and, following that, to dig our heels in and argue more forcefully for our position.

It's a rare person who is willing to set aside a belief and see an issue from the perspective of someone who disagrees. That's why many people read books and articles that support their preconceived notions and shun all others. Pride leads them to forget the imperfection of their human nature, forget that they can be wrong in their views. They persuade themselves that wondering anew about old issues will somehow jeopardize their individuality, and that changing their minds is dishonorable.

Such responses prevent us from growing in knowledge and wisdom. They are a mark, not of individuality, but of foolishness.

Good-Habit Builder

For the next few days, be alert for occasions when people disagree with you. The disagreement may be direct, as in the case where you express an idea and someone challenges it. Or it may be indirect, as in the case where you have not stated your view but realize, in hearing the other person's idea, that yours differs.

Whenever such occasions arise, pay close attention to your reactions. Notice the emotions you experience toward the person and the idea, what thoughts occur to you, and what you subsequently say and do. Decide whether you are well or poorly served by those reactions.

Resist External and Internal Pressures

One measure of individuality is how well we resist external pressures. These can be so subtle that we are unaware that they exist. Popular culture, for example, will often create a climate of opinion that disposes people to take a certain stand on an issue even when they lack the necessary information to make any judgment.

Two fairly typical cases are the Mapplethorpe photographs and 2 Live Crew's album, *As Nasty as They Want to Be*. When the late Robert Mapplethorpe's photographs were exhibited, some people found them obscene. Newspaper descriptions were at first circumspect, frequently saying little more than some of the work was "homoerotic." This was hardly enough to base a thoughtful judgment on. Nevertheless, editorial pages were filled with columns and letters supporting or condemning the artist's work, *presumably written in profound ignorance of the facts*.

Similarly, when the members of the rap group 2 Live Crew were arrested in Florida on obscenity charges, a month or more passed before anyone in the news media found the courage to publish even an edited version of the supposedly objectionable words. Yet that didn't prevent thousands of people from joining the debate in newspapers and magazines around the United States and, in many cases, expressing judgments about whether the court should return a guilty verdict.

Such reactions are reminiscent of Pavlov's famous dog, who was conditioned to drool when a bell was rung. For some, the bell was the liberal dogma that any development that bears even a remote association with censorship must be loudly denounced. For others, it was the conservative dogma that art must never deal with controversial themes.

Internal pressures threaten our individuality as much as external ones. Among the strongest internal pressures are our wishes and desires. Many a poor student has repeated "I'm doing well in school" so often that he or she came to believe it and was genuinely shocked at the end of the marking period. Many a suitor has persuaded himself that the girl he is attracted to really cares for him, despite seemingly undeniable evidence to the contrary. Alcoholics and chronic gamblers typically believe they can quit any time they want. And people who don't pay their debts manage to transform their guilt into resentment of the person who was kind enough to lend them money.

The more sensitive you are to the external and internal pressures working on your mind, the better you will be able to resist surrendering your individuality to them.

Good-Habit Builder

Recall some views you expressed to others in the past several weeks. Probe the circumstances in which you formed those ideas and decide to what extent, if any, you were reacting to external or internal pressures.

Take a Balanced View of Conformity

Some people believe that conformity is always bad and should therefore be avoided. As a means of preserving their individuality, they cultivate being different. If most of us speak, dress, or wear our hair one way, these people speak, dress, or wear their hair another. Whatever social conventions are widely accepted, they reject. Ironically, these efforts don't achieve individuality; they merely result in an alternate form of dependency. Mindless nonconformity is no better than mindless conformity.

Not all conformity is bad. We conform when we obey traffic signals, say hello instead of goodbye when we meet people, observe the rules of etiquette, and meet deadlines for income tax returns. In such cases conformity is reasonable; it ensures safety, makes relations with others more pleasant, and spares us legal difficulties.

Conformity is harmful only when it involves a surrender of judgment: when we do as others do, or as they tell us to do, rather than decide for ourselves. Why would anyone surrender judgment in this way? As a rule, because of laziness or an inordinate desire for approval.

There's nothing wrong with wanting other people's approval. Children should want to please their parents, marriage partners should want to please their mates, employees should want to please employers, and we all should want to maintain good relations with those with whom we work, worship, and share a neighborhood. But doing the right, the reasonable, the appropriate thing should always take precedence over this desire. Those who genuinely care for us would never want it otherwise.

Insecurity may lead us to believe that other people's judgments, particularly those of the majority, are necessarily wiser than our own and that fashion in its various forms is infallible. These ideas are mistaken. Even experts can err.

Fred Astaire is universally acclaimed as one of the finest dancers who ever graced the movie screen. Yet the official evaluation made after his first screen test was, "Can't act. Can't sing. Balding. Can dance a little."

Some years ago an individual decided to test the ability of publishers to recognize a masterpiece. He took the script of the famous movie *Casablanca*, made just enough changes, mainly of names and places, so that it wouldn't be easily recognized, and sent it off to a number of literary agents. Virtually every one of them pronounced it unworthy of publication.

About twenty years ago David Rosenhan conducted a study of mental hospitals, using eight normal, healthy adults. The eight appeared at twelve different mental hospitals with the same complaint—hearing mostly unclear voices and using the words "hollow," "empty," and "thud." Except for this lie, they gave true personal histories. All were quickly admitted and all but one were diagnosed as schizophrenic. Once admitted, all stopped faking symptoms and behaved sanely. Yet, once diagnosed, everything they did was regarded as a sign of emotional disorder. They were kept in the hospital an average of 19 days.[3]

If experts can make such blunders, the judgments of average people offer no guarantee of wisdom. And there is no magic in majorities. Similarly, fashion is far from infallible. Not only does it change suddenly and capriciously, but virtually anyone can make it change. A friend of mine grew up when the fashion in footwear was a particular brand of saddle shoes. One day in a moment of daring she purchased a pair of boys' brogues and boldly wore them to school. Apprehensive at first, she soon learned how capricious the prevailing fashion was. The other girls tripped over one another to follow her lead and buy boys' brogues.

To be an individual, you must make your own assessments. In matters of taste, such as clothing, hairstyle, and choice of automobiles, decide what you really like. In matters of judgment, such as the formation of beliefs, values, and positions on important issues, decide what is most reasonable. Have the humility to conform with others when honesty and good sense warrant; have the courage to resist conforming merely to avoid thinking or to gain others' approval.

Good-Habit Builder

Identify situations in which you have unwisely conformed, or situations in which you have unwisely resisted conforming. Decide how you should have thought, spoken, and acted in each of those situations.

4

Habits
for Efficiency

"Why can't I get things done? Before I finish one assignment at work, it seems two more are on my desk. When I go home at night, yesterday's chores are there to greet me. Often as not, I'm late paying my bills, and more than once I've had to file for an extension on my income tax. I have this picture of myself on a treadmill, always rushing but never really getting anyplace."

It's a common lament. Even if your situation is not this bad, you can probably identify with the feeling. Relatively few people have found a way to juggle their many responsibilities effectively.

The solution is to become more efficient. Efficiency, unfortunately, frightens many people. They see it as cold, regimented, and mechanical and fear it will make their lives grim and joyless. Others fear it will make them do everything too quickly and thereby diminish the quality of their performance. Both notions are mistaken.

By enabling us to do more things in the same amount of time, efficiency creates time. Minutes saved here and there become hours over the course of several days or weeks. That means more time to devote to important activities, more time to enjoy life.

Determine How You Waste Time

In the late 1950s, as a young industrial engineer, I was responsible for doing time-and-motion studies and setting work standards in a large mail-order house. Conducting such a study entails determining what motions are most economical and least tiring and measuring the time each takes. The engineer must be alert for unnecessary motions and unrelated activities.

My experiences quickly led me to three conclusions. Few people think about the way they do a job; they simply fall into a performance pattern and continue it, however inefficient it may be. Also, most people are unaware of the extent to which distractions and interruptions, external and self-generated, affect their performance. Finally, many people squander time without realizing it.

Today the average worker reportedly wastes up to a third of each workday, for a total of sixteen weeks annually. Though in some cases the waste may be intentional, in the great majority of cases it is simply a result of poor habits. The resulting deficit in productivity is certainly a factor in the relatively high cost of goods and services in this country and the growing difficulty of meeting the challenge of foreign competition.

But the loss is not confined to the workplace. The habit of inefficiency often extends into personal lives, creating problems in marital relationships and parenting, problems that are compounded when children imitate their parents' bad example.

The first step in becoming more efficient is to find out how you waste time. Here are the most common ways.

Performing Unnecessary Tasks

The several employees who had spent, in total, about ten hours a week for the last three years creating a re-

port for the home office had been told it was important.
I wondered, and so I asked the accounting manager, who
confirmed its importance. Yet when I checked with the
home office, I found the report had been discontinued
more than a year earlier—but no one had bothered to
communicate that fact to our branch.

The lesson in this case, one you can put to good use, is
this: What may seem important may not be. And what
was important a month or a year ago may no longer be so.

Performing Necessary Tasks Inefficiently

Extra movement, like walking or bending or reaching,
takes time. So does using five or six steps when we could
accomplish the same task in three or four, or taking a
separate trip for each of several errands when with a
little planning a single trip would suffice.

Performing Tasks We Could Assign to Others

Executives sometimes do tasks themselves that their
secretaries or clerks should do. The executives reason,
usually incorrectly, that they are being self-sufficient or
that it would take too much time to explain what they
want done. Parents sometimes take the same approach
with their children and unnecessarily burden themselves
with activities that consume hundreds of hours annually.

Tolerating Distractions

If our attention is not focused on what we are doing,
we are more likely to experience time-consuming false
starts and mental lapses and to make mistakes. It may
not be possible to eliminate all impediments to concentration; a receptionist can't avoid greeting people when
they enter the office. Yet many can be eliminated. For

example, a radio or tape player can be turned off, or a desk can be turned away from a busy aisle.

Waiting to Do Something

Waiting is an unavoidable part of contemporary life. On the way to work, we wait for the bus or train or carpool driver; if we drive ourselves, we wait for stoplights and traffic jams. When we arrive at work, we wait for meetings to begin or for clients to call. When we go to the doctor or dentist, we wait in the aptly named "waiting room." We wait on lines in the supermarket. And if we have children, we wait to pick them up from school or dance lessons or newspaper routes. Most of this waiting time is unproductive.

Outside Interruptions

The telephone is a necessity in this age of communication, and it can save us time. However, it usually tends to decrease our efficiency. Every time we answer the phone, we take time from what we have been doing. Then, when we finish the conversation, we must spend extra time refocusing our thoughts. The same kind of time loss occurs whenever we turn from paperwork to dealing with a customer or co-worker.

Self-Distraction

Off-the-subject thoughts enter everyone's consciousness from time to time. If we fail to exercise self-control, or if we go out of our way to indulge in daydreaming, we can waste a great deal of time staring off into space, enjoying our reverie but accomplishing nothing while doing so.

Engaging in Idle Conversation

Much of the conversation that occurs in the workplace is unnecessary and unproductive. Discussion of personal problems, world and local affairs, sports, and experiences with clients, supervisors, and subordinates can prevent us from doing our jobs.

Extended Workday Breaks

The coffee break is a time-honored tradition. Properly used, it sends us back to work refreshed and eager to take up where we left off. But unless we are vigilant, ten or fifteen minutes can easily extend to twenty or thirty, twice a day. Add that time to the time spent preparing to go to lunch, having lunch, and settling back to work after lunch, and our relaxation time can exceed two and a half hours a day. That's almost one third of the average workday.

Good-Habit Builder

Review your daily routine. List every activity during every waking hour of the day, even the minor unscheduled activities that take only five or ten minutes. Underline those activities in which you are less efficient than you might be and estimate the total time you waste as a result.

Free Yourself of Unnecessary Activities

Your review of your daily routine undoubtedly disclosed some time spent in unnecessary activities. Certain of these activities, you may decide, are worth continuing because they bring you pleasure. Fair enough. I know a retired science teacher who is a prodigious record keeper. He faithfully logs morning and evening temperatures and weather conditions. And his baseball records would delight a statistician. He has time to spare and derives enjoyment from these activities.

Similarly, a former neighbor keeps what might be called a journal of pain. He has accumulated in this volume every medical condition he has suffered, every treatment undergone, every medication prescribed, and virtually every pain he has experienced in recent years. Since he is over eighty, the last category is constantly expanding. His journal is his only hobby; it gives him something to do with his time and, though occasionally leading to morbid preoccupation, it probably saves him from greater morbidity.

Both these individuals are better off continuing these unnecessary activities than curtailing them. But that is not the case with everyone.

A professor I taught with some years ago was a compulsive comparison shopper. He spent hours poring over the grocery store ads and making copious notes about how many cents cheaper canned vegetables or paper products were in store C, over stores A and B. When his analysis was complete and his teaching duties were fulfilled, he would drive from store to store to buy the best bargains. Since he lived in a rural area, he often drove twenty miles one way to take advantage of a sale.

This man obviously spent hours each week in this activity and undoubtedly saved some money. Just how much is debatable, because he drove a big station wagon and gas was costly. But he also kept lamenting the fact that he couldn't finish a book project that was long overdue. I don't think he ever saw the connection between squandering time on shopping and lacking time for an important project.

Considerably more common than the professor's preoccupation is the habit of seizing every opportunity for conversation. Here's how it typically works. Sam goes to work early because he has an important project to finish before the end of the week. Just as he is about to enter the office, he meets Bill and talks to him for ten minutes about the football games played over the weekend. About an hour later his assistant asks him a question and, after answering it, Sam says, "Some game the Vikings played yesterday, right?" And another ten minutes expires.

At ten-thirty, Sam joins Mary and Tony for coffee. Their conversation ranges over the trouble in the Middle East, the dearth of viable political candidates, and the increasing crime problem in their city. Coffee break over, Mary takes her leave, but Sam and Tony linger to discuss football. Twelve minutes later, Tony excuses himself and Sam returns to the office.

At eleven-fifty-five the phone rings. It's Larry asking Sam to go to lunch. Sam looks at his watch and sighs, says, "Noon already? Where has the morning gone?" and tells Larry he'll meet him at the restaurant in ten minutes.

Let's add up the time Sam spent in conversation unrelated to work: thirty-two minutes' worth, most of it repeating the same ideas over and over. If the afternoon goes the same way, there will be more repetition and more time wasted.

The solution to Sam's problem is to curtail the unnecessary conversation. Should he talk during coffee breaks and lunch? Of course. But he should stifle the urge at other times. When he meets people in the hallway, he should exchange pleasantries and say, "See you later." That one habit would gain him over an hour a day and over two hundred hours annually!

Good-Habit Builder

Examine your daily list of activities. Review those you underlined and determine which of them are partly or wholly unnecessary. Resolve to eliminate them. Over the next week or two be alert for the old habit to re-assert itself and, when it does, resist it.

Delegate Some Responsibilities

Parents of large families can testify that many hands make light work. These people have usually been driven to this truth by necessity. Initially, they may have been tempted to do everything themselves—after all, it takes time and patience to teach children to do dishes, wash and iron clothes, and perform a hundred other chores. Nevertheless, as their families grew in size, there was no viable alternative. And so they discovered how much more sensible it is to invest the time in teaching the oldest child, letting that child teach the next, and so on, than to do everything themselves.

The responsibilities of business and professional people multiply over the years much as the responsibilities of parents of a growing family. Delegating responsibilities makes sense for them too.

If you are a workaholic or simply someone who takes great pride in your work, your first thought may be, But I can't delegate any of my responsibilities. They're too important to be entrusted to anyone else. Or you may think, Perhaps when I have the time, I will delegate some responsibilities, but I just don't have the time now. Don't succumb to such thinking. Reason with yourself as follows:

If I were incapacitated for a month or more, someone else would have to do all my work. And if a capable person was chosen, he or she would learn to do a competent job without my guidance. Surely I can entrust a small part of my work to someone *under* my guidance.

Or:

What's the sense of telling myself I'll wait until I have time if lack of time is my problem to begin with? If I

make a little time now to delegate some of my responsibilities, I'll save a lot of time in the future.

Good-Habit Builder

Don't *consider* whether you will delegate some responsibilities. Take it as a given that you will. Just decide what
specific ones and to whom you'll delegate them. For example, if you are a teacher, consider delegating to your
students; if you are a single parent working alone in your
home, consider delegating to your child. To be sure you
follow through, let the person know of your decision and
begin your instructions today.

Limit Your Accessibility

The more accessible you are to others, the more obstacles to efficiency you are likely to encounter. An executive who answers her own phone will experience
more interruptions than one who doesn't. A parent always available to his teenage children is sure to have less
time to himself than one who is not so available. A college student who is always visible to roommates is certain to experience more distractions than one who is not.

Total inaccessibility is not possible for most people;
even if it were, they probably wouldn't want it. What
you should aim for is a reasonable gain in time spent
without distraction. Here are some ways to get it.

If you are an executive or a professional person, determine what time of day—early morning, say, or late afternoon—is the most productive time for you. Then tell
your secretary, if you have one, that you are not to be
disturbed during that time. Instruct the secretary to say
you are not available to speak on the phone then and to
take names and telephone numbers. You can return the
call later at a more convenient time.

If you do not have a secretary, invest in an answering

machine and use it during the time you wish to remain inaccessible. For maximum solitude, turn the sound down so that you don't hear your taped message or the caller's voice. Or, if you prefer, monitor incoming calls and take only the most urgent ones. Return the other calls later.

If your business involves seeing clients in your office, block some "inaccessible" time out of your schedule. For example, if your practice has been to have your office open to clients from 9 to 5 every day and closed from 12 to 1 P.M., you may decide to reserve the first two hours for yourself and schedule office hours from 11 to 5. (By eating lunch in the office, you gain two hours of time and only curtail office availability by a single hour.)

If you are a parent who does not work outside the home, let your family know what time you are reserving for yourself and make it clear that you are not to be disturbed then except in cases of emergency. (Many people get up an hour or two earlier than the rest of the family and use that time as their own.) If you are a college student, find a place on campus where you can minimize the chance of interruption—the library, for example, or an empty classroom.

Good-Habit Builder

Decide at what time of day you are most productive. Consider the foregoing ways to limit your accessibility, as well as any others you can think of. Choose the ones that will work best for you and begin implementing them today.

Plan Each Day

An unusually efficient working mother I know has classified recurring work around the house in three categories—daily, weekly, and monthly. Every task is assigned a particular time in her busy schedule. Each morning, a single glance at the schedule lets her know what needs to be done. She also has a monthly menu that serves as an aid to grocery shopping and saves her from wondering what to have for dinner.

For nonrecurring tasks, such as special projects at work or "must do's" for tomorrow or the next day, she keeps another list. As each day progresses and she receives an assignment or decides that something must be done (buying a birthday card, calling her son's teacher, scheduling a professional meeting), she jots it down on this list, where possible fitting it into a time slot that meets the demands of the activity and her biorhythms. Being a morning person, she tries to schedule more intellectually demanding activities early in the day.

Most efficient people employ some variation of this approach. Experience has taught them that a planned day is usually a more productive day.

Good-Habit Builder

Make a list of your recurring tasks. Decide the best time of day and, if possible, the most appropriate day of the week or month to do each. Post this list in a conspicuous place.

Next, make a list of tomorrow's activities. For any task that places a special demand on your concentration, patience, or thinking skill, choose a time when you can perform it most effectively. Continue this list making tomorrow and thereafter.

Do Unpleasant Things First

How many times have you gone through a day, a week, or even longer saying to yourself from time to time, "I've got to do that. I should have done it before this. It's overdue, but how I hate to do it!" That uncompleted task is a constant burden. Whatever you do, wherever you go, it goes with you, ready to be recalled and accompanied by an unpleasant feeling, a wringing of hands, and a feeble promise to complete it soon.

If you've had this experience, you know how satisfying it is when, at long last, you stop avoiding the unpleasant task and finally perform it. You feel an instant sense of relief and may say to yourself, "That really wasn't so bad; next time I won't delay so long." Unfortunately, the habit of procrastination can easily defeat the good intention.

There is a simple solution to this problem: Start off every day doing the unpleasant tasks first. If you hate making your bed, don't wait until bedtime to make it; you'll have carried an unmade bed on your mind for sixteen hours. Instead, make it the moment you roll out of it in the morning. And if you dread telephoning that client to say his project is going to be delayed, don't wait until the end of the day or week to call. If you do, every hour between now and then will be darkened by the thought of having to call him. Instead, call him the moment you learn the bad news.

One reward for doing unpleasant tasks first each day is that you're guaranteed to continue each day with a sense of relief and accomplishment. In addition, once you're free of dread, everything you do for the rest of the day will seem less burdensome. Your enjoyment of your job may increase, and in this day when reports of people hating their work are common, that's no small benefit.

Good-Habit Builder

Make a list of the things you most hate doing and usually procrastinate about. Include activities at home as well as at work. Post the list in a conspicuous place—on the bathroom mirror, for example—as a reminder. And whenever you find yourself saying, "I've got to do such-

and-such when I get a chance," stop everything and do it then.

Use Waiting to Advantage

You arrive at the dentist's office and the receptionist announces, "Doctor is running a little late today." You plunk down in the only available chair and survey the scene. Six other people in the waiting room. If all of them are ahead of you and each takes thirty minutes. . . . You groan in contemplation of the wait.

Waiting is a terrible business, whether it's for a professional to keep your appointment, someone to arrive for a meeting, or some event to happen, such as your plane to break out of the holding pattern and land so you can race to make your connection. Time drags; you cast nervous glances at your watch and mentally check off all the things you want to be doing. By some perverse law, the more important the activities not being accomplished, the longer you have to wait.

It doesn't have to be that way, though. Viewed more positively, every occasion of waiting is an opportunity to get things done. How many tasks could you have accomplished in that dentist's waiting room? Here's a partial list:

Plan your menus for the next week
Create some unusual dessert recipes
Make out your Christmas card list
Brainstorm for gift ideas
Balance your checkbook
Jot down ideas for dealing with a personal problem—
    a foundering relationship, for example
Knit or do cross-stitch
Draft some business or personal letters
Rough out a business proposal
Do some memorandums to superiors, subordinates, or
    clients

Read a book you've put aside for a spare moment
Entertain possible career moves
Consider various hobbies you might pursue

Different kinds of waiting suggest different possibilities. If you drive to and from work and find yourself waiting in traffic, you can use an audio tape to increase your understanding of some aspect of your field or to improve your professional skills. Or you can use the tape recorder to brainstorm aloud for solutions to a problem.

Waiting during commercial breaks on television is a good time for making out your budget, paying your bills, ironing your shirts or dresses, shining your shoes, filing your nails, or doing calisthenics.

With a modest investment in ingenuity, waiting will never again be a waste of time.

Good-Habit Builder

List all the occasions in a typical week when you have to wait for someone or something. For each of those occasions, think of as many activities as you can to put that time to good use.

Change Activities to Maintain Your Pace

Even activities we find interesting can become boring when we work at them too long at one sitting. And the moment they become boring, the chance for distractions and loss of productivity increases dramatically.

There is no single tolerance level. One person may be able to work for hours at an activity with no loss of efficiency. Another may last for only fifteen minutes. One determining factor is whether or not we like what we're doing; enjoyment increases tolerance. Another factor is our attention span. Popular culture has tended to hinder the development of both.

Our grandparents arguably derived more enjoyment from their work and leisure activities because they were less concerned that every activity be exciting and instantly gratifying. In addition, their attention span was allowed to mature, whereas television—with its frequent commerical interruptions, its technological devices, and its hype, glitter, and quick scene shifts—has prevented ours from maturing.

Changing activities now and then can prevent loss of interest or concentration from affecting your performance. Keep two or three projects available. When you sense yourself losing attention or your pace is slowing, set aside the project you are working on and take up another. Or turn to a different aspect of your first project.

A writer, for example, might stop writing a chapter of a book and spend some time proofreading an earlier chapter or doing some background reading for a later one. A commercial artist might turn from the finishing detail work on a poster to rough-sketch a brochure for another client.

At times a more dramatic change of activity may be necessary, such as switching from a mental to a physical activity. You might stand and do calisthenics or take a walk around the block or read a newspaper. By experimenting with different activities, you will learn the kind of changes that work best for you and the minimum length of time needed to regain your concentration.

Good-Habit Builder

Monitor your daily activities and note when you begin to lose your concentration. Look for general patterns as well as isolated instances. (You may find that certain activities or certain times of the day are especially problematic.) Experiment a little and try to find activity changes that restore your concentration without diminishing your productivity.

5

Habits
for Creativity

Creativity is a mental process for producing ideas that are both uncommon and uncommonly good, ideas that solve problems and resolve issues.

Studies show that 95 percent of us have significant creativity in early childhood, but most of us abandon it before we reach our teens. Only 2 percent of adults demonstrate the characteristics of creativity.[4] What makes people lose their creativity? Parents who grow tired of children's questions—"Why, Mommy? Why, Daddy?"—will communicate their displeasure, verbally or otherwise. Also, the schools' emphasis on possessing knowledge but not using it forces students into a passive role by giving them information to memorize rather than guiding them to discovery and application.

Another reason creativity withers is that people are suspicious of it. This is the case with some conservative Christians, who reason that creativity is "not of God" and therefore a threat to our spiritual welfare. Such thinking is unfortunate and mistaken. We were made in God's image and likeness, spiritual beings with intellects and wills, and given dominion over all creation. Why would God have given us minds if not to use them in

His service? Refusing to nurture and use our God-given capacity is not a virtue. At the very least, it is a tragedy; in some cases, a sin.

Can creativity be used against God's purpose? Of course. But so can any other of God's gifts. That is hardly a reason to reject them. To treat the mind as nothing more than a container for information is to deny our nature and to doubt God's wisdom.

Research reveals that the creativity most people abandon in childhood is not really lost but merely hidden and can be regained by developing the right habits. Good sense urges us to develop those habits.

Put Ignorance to Work for You

As young children we were acutely aware of our ignorance, so we were open to learning. We asked questions incessantly. "Mommy, why is Bobby's hair darker than mine?" "Daddy, why does it get dark at night?" "Why don't animals talk to us?" "Why do children go to school?" "Why do I like some stories better than others?" Why? Why? Why? The world was a wondrous place, and every ant, every flower, every mud puddle was fascinating.

As we grew older, however, we came to realize that not knowing is considered shameful. People who don't know are called ugly names, like idiot, moron, and imbecile. It became more important for us to hide our ignorance, to pretend to know, and, whenever we had the chance, to parade our knowledge before others. Thus telling displaced asking and curiosity was stilled.

By the time we become adults, the world has become, for many of us, a rather boring place. We have grown comfortable with our little store of knowledge. Like an old shoe, it fits well. We feel no sense of deprivation, no need to explore more widely or probe more deeply. We are prisoners of contentment.

The longer we live in this state of mind, the more fearful and resentful we are likely to be of the new and the unfamiliar. We will resist ideas we have not heard before, and in so doing we will oppose other people's creativity and stifle our own. After all, every discovery, every invention, every original idea is by definition new and unfamiliar.

It is just such resistance to change that has retarded progress through the ages. Virtually every idea or invention that proved a boon to society was denounced as radical, even satanic. The list includes the automobile and the airplane, the umbrella, the sewing maching, anesthesia, eyeglasses, indoor plumbing, social security, mass education, and women's suffrage.

The popular notion is that science and technology are based on the scientific method. But scientists know there is something more fundamental—the scientific attitude, a sense of wonder plus an earnest desire to discover the nature of things, how they work, why they are as they are, whether they might be different and, if so, with what effects on the world. Many researchers observed the inhibiting effects of molds on staphylococcus colony growth, but only Alexander Fleming was curious about the phenomeonon and wondered how it might be used to conquer disease.

Nor is this attitude peculiar to science. It is central to every field of knowledge. And it is indispensable to progress.

How can you begin to develop and nurture this attitude? By changing your perspective on ignorance, seeing its value, making it your ally. Stop pretending that you know when you don't know. Overcome your concern that someone might laugh at your lack of knowledge. Instead of suppressing questions, ask them. The search for knowledge begins in the acknowledgment of ignorance; unasked questions never get answered.

Good-Habit Builder

Today, if someone raises a subject you are unfamiliar with, say "I'm not familiar with this; could you give me some background on it?" If you don't understand a point someone makes, request an explanation. If someone expresses an opinion without explaining the reasoning that led to it, inquire about that reasoning. Be ready for an inner voice saying, "Don't ask; people might think you stupid or naive," and if it does, ignore it.

Look for Other People's Creativity

Many years ago, when my first house was being built, the builder asked me, "What color roofing shingles do you want? I recommend white."

"White?" I said in disbelief. "I've never heard of white shingles." It was true. I had never, to my knowledge, ever seen white shingles on a house.

"No need to decide just yet," he explained. "But the next time you're out driving, look for white roofs. See how many you find."

I did as he suggested and found that virtually every second house had a white roof. I hadn't noticed them before only because I hadn't been looking for them.

That's the way it is with creativity. Though you may not have noticed, it lies all around you. Look on your desk and you'll undoubtedly find pencils and pens, paper clips, a stapler, transparent tape, a jackknife, rubber bands, scissors, a clock, a telephone, books, envelopes, your checkbook, postage stamps. Every one of these is the wonderful product of someone's creativity.

All the rooms in your house bear similar silent testimony to creativity, as does every place you go outside. The supermarket, the library, the discount store, the football stadium, the school, the office building, the fast-food restaurant, the shopping mall, the television studio—all these places are not only filled with examples of creativity, they are themselves creative ideas.

The most wonderful thing about creativity is that opportunities for it never diminish. How many different kinds of writing instruments have been developed since someone first scratched one stone with another? How many kinds of lights since the first torch? How many kinds of beds, shoes, cameras, boats, hats, baskets, food recipes?

The more you notice and appreciate the creativity around you, the more aware you will be of opportunities to use creativity to improve your own life and the lives of others.

Good-Habit Builder

For the next twenty-four hours, look for examples of creativity at home, at work, and in traveling from place to place. Look, too, in the newspapers and on TV news programs. List all the examples of creativity you find, both recent and older. Include products and services, concepts, processes, and procedures.

Recognize and Deal with Problems

The college president says "At this time George Miller, our Vice President for Business Affairs, will explain the new budget."

George comes to the front of the auditorium, puts a transparency on the overhead projector, and begins speaking. "I know that those of you in the back of the auditorium probably can't read these figures, but . . . " His voice trails off for a second, and then he launches into his discussion of the budget.

What happened here occurs frequently, not only in education but in business as well. A problem exists—in this case, people in the back of the room can't see.

George knew it existed; he even called attention to it. But he did nothing about it. (The solution to the problem is simple; he could have implemented it before he left his office. It is to enlarge the important section of the transparency or provide a handout of the report and eliminate the transparency altogether.)

Recognizing problems when they occur is important. But it is not sufficient. We must also address them and find solutions. The best way to be sure you do so is to approach problems aggressively. Instead of waiting until they affect others or become crises, seek them out. Examine every aspect of your job from time to time and look for indications of potential problems.

If your work involves a process or procedure, such as teaching, counseling people, processing forms in an office, or providing customers with a service, ask yourself these questions:

> Could the process be made clearer to those who must know, including employees and customers?
> Could it be made safer?
> Could it be made more convenient (for example, done at a more appropriate time)?
> Could it be made simpler (for example, by eliminating some steps)?
> Could it be made faster—where, exactly, are the delays?—or, if speed is undesirable, slower?
> Could it be made more economical, so that more people can afford it?
> Could it be made less stressful, more comfortable for those involved?

If your work involves designing, manufacturing, or handling a product, ask yourself these questions:

> Could it be made safer?
> Could it be more convenient to obtain or to use?
> Could it be more durable (in itself or in its packaging)?

Could it be made less expensive (to make or deliver)?
Could it be made more readily available?
Could it be delivered more quickly?
Could its performance be improved (making it last longer, serve a dual purpose, or work more efficiently or effectively)?
Could its appearance be improved?
Could it be made more compatible with other things?
Could its name be improved?

These questions about processes and products needn't be limited to what you do in the workplace. They apply to what you do at home, as well.

Good-Habit Builder

Consider various processes and products you are involved with at work or at home. Identify as many actual or potential problems as you can.

Examine Problems from Many Perspectives

Some years ago the owners of a Texas high-rise office building received complaints about the slowness of the elevators. Eager to solve the problem, they called in engineers, who observed the number of people waiting for elevators at various times of the day and determined the average wait time. Their recommendation was to sink a new elevator shaft, a costly undertaking.

Hoping there might be an easier solution, the owners next turned to an unlikely source: psychologists. After studying the problem, the psychologists proposed that the owners surround the lobby elevators with mirrors, on the theory that time would pass more quickly for people if they were able to look at themselves and check their clothing and appearance while waiting for the elevator. This inexpensive alternative was implemented, and it worked!

The engineers saw an engineering problem and sought an engineering solution: How can this elevator system get people to their destinations faster? The psychologists, on the other hand, saw a human problem and sought a human solution: How can the wait be made to *seem* shorter to people? We all tend to view problems a certain way, a way that reflects our training and interests. (The generalists among us have a certain advantage over the specialists: a wider frame of reference.)

Since the best and most creative solution to a problem may lie outside our usual focus, we need to find a way to broaden our perspective. One effective way is to ask "How can?" questions. Let's say your problem is that your company parking lot is often filled when you get to work. Your first thought might be, How can I get the company to enlarge the parking lot? Pressing yourself to consider other perspectives, you come up with these possibilities: How can I get a parking space before the lot is filled? or, How can I find a parking place outside the company lot but within walking distance? or, How can I get to work without driving?

Notice that each new perspective points not just to other solutions but to other *kinds* of solutions, kinds you might otherwise overlook. In this case, those solutions include arriving at work earlier (and perhaps getting approval to have your working hours adjusted accordingly), joining a car pool, and renting a space in someone's driveway for a nominal fee.

Good-Habit Builder

Select a current problem and view it from a variety of perspectives, asking as many and varied "How can?" questions as possible. Decide what answers represent the best solutions to the problem.

Enrich Your Thinking

Seeing a problem from many perspectives will always generate more ideas than seeing it from a single perspective. But if you are able to produce only a single answer for each "How can?" question you ask, you will still be idea poor. Moreover, your answers are likely to be uncreative. Early ideas are usually the most common ideas, tried and *un*true, and therefore unsatisfactory solutions to your problem.

There are a number of proven ways to enrich your thinking. The most basic is simply to extend your idea production. It helps if you set goals for yourself, saying, for example, "I will produce at least twenty-five possibilities before I make my selection," and making yourself do so.

This may sound artificial and contrived, but it works. At the beginning of my college course in creative thinking, most students could produce only a few ideas for each problem. I might ask them to think of names for a seafood restaurant, or titles for a composition, or ways of dealing with a pesky neighbor. The next day I would go around the room asking how many ideas they produced. The number ranged from 3 to 5 or 10; an occasional student would have 15.

I would then explain that we tend unconsciously to limit the number of our ideas and by conscious effort can produce many more than we thought possible. After a few assignments, the same students who had been unable to produce more than 5 ideas were producing 50 or 100.

Another way to enrich your thinking is to suspend all judgment. When searching for solutions to our problems, we frequently patrol the edge of our consciousness and, the moment an idea appears, we judge it. If it doesn't seem worthy, we immediately discard it.

What criterion do we use to judge? Whether it seems appropriate or sensible. The trouble is, at first appearance the most creative ideas are likely to seem inappropriate or foolish. Only after we have gotten used to them are we able to see their worth.

Kim and Barbara worked for the same boss, a difficult person who bombarded them with unfair and withering sarcasm and personal insults. A blowup seemed inevitable, in which one or both would surely lose their jobs, so they brainstormed to find a solution to their problem. One idea seemed totally ridiculous when they thought of it, but fortunately they didn't discard it because it proved to be the best solution. The idea was to turn the boss's attacks into a competition. Whoever was insulted was awarded a point; at the end of the week the points were tallied and the one with the higher score got a free dinner from the other.

Judging ideas as soon as we produce them not only deprives us of some good ideas, it also slows idea production, sometimes stopping it completely. One idea can lead to another, but only if we let it do so by postponing all judgment.

A third way to enrich your thinking is to stimulate your imagination, using one or more of the following strategies.

Force uncommon responses. After you have produced some common ideas, press yourself to produce some unusual ones. (Don't worry if this effort produces twenty silly or outrageous ideas for every valuable one. The occasional good one will be worth the effort.)

Use analogy. Gutenberg got the idea for the printing press by observing a winepress in operation. He was thinking analogically. Examining your problem closely and asking, "What situation does it remind me of? What is it like?" may stimulate your imagination.

Visualize the solution. Try imagining the problem solved and asking what the situation would look like then. For example, if the problem is how to gain more room in your house without spending a fortune, create a mental picture of how your house would look if it were enlarged. Visualize all the rooms. Would each room be larger? Would rooms be added? If so, in what part of the house? If there are several possibilities for change, which one would be most economical?

By using this approach a young couple I know came up with an idea for adding much-needed space at modest expense. Their two-car garage was attached to the kitchen, so they converted half the garage into a dining room and extra bedroom.

Use free association. Formal education often teaches us to classify knowledge too rigidly: "This is scientific knowledge, that is literary, the other is social, and none must ever be joined." Actually, many creative ideas are a result of such joining. By relaxing control of your mind and letting one idea suggest another, you can sometimes break down the artificial barriers between subjects and gain an insight.

Look for unusual combinations. Sometimes the most creative idea is one that combines two or more things not usually combined. The miner's cap (a hat plus a flashlight) and the wheelchair (a seat plus a moving vehicle) are examples of unusual combinations that resulted from creative thinking.

Good-Habit Builder

Select a problem you have had difficulty solving. Resolve to produce at least twenty-five possible solutions for it. Start by listing all the solutions you have thought of before. Then press yourself to think of some unusual ones and write them down as well. Resist the impulse to judge each idea as you think of it; don't worry if an idea seems too silly or unworkable to consider. Next, ask what other situation the present problem or situation reminds you of, and consider what insights the resulting analogy suggests. Try to visualize what the situation will look like when the problem is solved, and examine that visualization for clues to solving the problem. To produce additional ideas, review the ideas on your list and ask what associations each brings to mind. Finally, consider whether two or more ideas could be combined to produce an even better solution to the problem.

View Frustrations as Challenges

Industrialist Alex Osborn tells about the young man seeking his first job at a large department store. When he arrived at the personnel office, he was turned away because there were already too many applicants. Instead of accepting defeat, the young man merely asked himself, "How can I get through to the personnel director and demonstrate that it's in his interest to hire me?"

His solution was to walk through the store, observing where service might be improved. Then he telephoned the personnel director. "I want a job," he explained, "so I just spent the last two hours looking for places I might help. I found ten where I could help right now. May I come up and discuss them with you?" He not only got the interview, he got the job!

Most people would deal very differently with the frustration the young man faced. They'd walk away mumbling to themselves about their bad luck and seize every opportunity to share their self-pity with others. How often have you entered the lounge or cafeteria at work and heard people grumbling about someone or something. "She's so infuriating!" "Why don't they do something about . . . ?" "I'm fed up with . . . " Whining, denunciation, and griping about everything imaginable—people, places, procedures, products, and services—represent a sizable part of everyday conversation and, presumably, everyday mental activity.

Playing "Ain't It Awful?" doesn't solve problems, it merely spreads gloom. It's hard to believe people engage in it because they enjoy feeling depressed. A more reasonable explanation is that they don't know what else to do with their frustrations. Creative achievers, on the other hand, do know. They treat them as challenges to their ingenuity.

One evening in 1950, Francis McNamara was entertaining clients at a restaurant. When he went to pay the check, he discovered that he had left his wallet at home. His response to this embarrassing experience might have been to feel sorry for himself ("Ain't it awful, poor me") or play "If Only" ("If only I'd put the wallet in my pocket when I changed my trousers; if only I'd checked before I left home"). But instead he did something creative—he invented the credit card.

In 1907 Arthur Scott was already well established as a toilet tissue manufacturer. One day he received a defective shipment; the paper was too thick to be used for tissue. Instead of bemoaning the situation, Scott viewed it as a challenge. "How can I use this thicker paper?" he asked. And the answer—as disposable hand towels—created a new market for his company and offered the public a useful new product.

Ole Evinrude had rowed his girl to a picnic on an island in Lake Michigan. When she said she'd enjoy some ice cream, he rowed two and a half miles back to shore to get it. By the time he rowed back, it had melted and he felt foolish. But he was also spurred to solve the problem: How can a rowboat be made to travel faster than a man can row? He subsequently invented the outboard motor and founded the company that bears his name.

L. L. Bean was dissatisfied with both rubber boots and

leather boots. The former were too hot and sweaty; the latter leaked. So he found a way to combine the best features of both: He stitched a rubber bottom onto a leather top and created the first product for the famous mail-order company that bears his name.

The engineer who made a batch of glue that wouldn't stick very well could have cursed and thrown it away. Instead he asked how that glue could be used . . . and proceeded to invent the Post-It note pad.

Before 1980 all computers were incompatible. That was a source of frustration to countless computer users, including William Gates. But he did something about it. He devised a workable system that could be used in most computers. That system, which has become the industry standard, is the MicroSoft Disk Operating System, better known by the abbreviation MS-DOS.

Dave Ellis, president of College Survival, Inc., noticed that people attending conferences and seminars tend to sit in the back, making it difficult for speakers to engage them fully. So at his conferences he puts a ribbon on the back seven or eight rows until the front ones are filled. He also noticed that the typical name tag uses type too small to be read even from two or three feet away. So he has the first names of his conferees typed in oversized letters on their tags.

When her thirteen-year-old daughter was killed by a drunken hit-and-run driver, Candy Lightner was not only heartbroken but outraged as well; the driver had four prior DWI arrests. Eager to turn her emotion into meaningful action, she wondered, How can this tragic scenario be prevented from occurring again and again? Her answer was to found MADD (Mothers Against Drunk Driving).

Seeing frustrations as challenges transforms negative experiences into opportunities for achievement. And it turns potentially harmful emotions into motivation to succeed. This habit will enable you to draw strength from circumstances that others are defeated by and to retain optimism and confidence long after others have succumbed to bitterness and cynicism.

Good-Habit Builder

List the complaints you have heard others make, or have made yourself, in the last few days. Separate those you can do something about, directly or indirectly, from those you can't.

Consider each complaint as a problem. In other words, see it from as many perspectives as you can, framing a "How can?" question for each. Then apply your creativity and produce as many solutions as possible. Select the best one and apply it.

Make Good Things Better

"Leave well enough alone" and "If it ain't broke, don't fix it" are common perspectives on reality. But that is not the view of creative people. They are constantly on the alert for ways to make good things better. "Innovation is the competitive weapon of the winning performer," says Donald K. Clifford, Jr., president of Threshold Management. Successful companies, he notes, "innovate early and often, creating new markets, new products and services, and new ways of doing business."

Famous restaurateur Howard Johnson, originally known for his ice cream, was continually experimenting with new ideas. In all, he developed twenty-eight different flavors. Nor was product innovation his only area of achievement. He was also the first restaurateur to franchise his business.

Gerhard Mennen, founder of the company that bears his name, was first known for his talcum powder. After spending several years finding the right formula for his powder, he could have sat back and enjoyed his success.

The public was satisfied with his product, but he wasn't. He decided the cardboard box he (and his competitors) used for the powder wasn't good enough, so he devised a special metal can. Then he introduced perforated holes in the can so the powder could be shaken out. Later, he developed an airtight seam and a twist cover to keep the powder pure in storage.

When Joyce Hall, founder of Hallmark greeting cards, began the business, greeting cards covered only two occasions: Christmas and Valentine's Day. His first contribution was to create a friendship card with the message *I'd like to be the kind of friend you've been to me.* (That card is still a top seller today, three quarters of a century later.) Never content to leave well enough alone, Hall continued to identify new "sending situations" and create a line of cards for each. By the time he retired in 1966, he had identified and marketed in three thousand different situations.

Great achievers recognize a truth that popular opinion overlooks: Because nothing of human invention is ever perfect, everything can be improved. This insight drives their creativity, fanning their excitement, motivating them not just to make bad things good but also to make good things better.

Every well-run company applies this insight in its research and development department, which constantly explores ways to improve the company's products or services, regardless of how good they are already. The creative people who work in R & D conceive the new designs and features for virtually everything you buy or use. By approaching your daily activities as they do theirs, you can inspire yourself to use your creativity more fully.

Good-Habit Builder

Think of at least one activity you do reasonably well and ask how you can improve your performance. List as many possibilities as you can and put the best ones to work for you.

Leapfrog Others' Achievements

Dennis was sitting at the breakfast table reading the morning paper when he first noticed that the pictures and descriptions of two missing children were printed on the side of the milk carton. A public service organization employee, Dennis was impressed with the idea. "Such an obvious idea," he thought. "Now why didn't I think of that?" He asked the question rhetorically, assuming it was unanswerable, and returned to reading his paper.

Dennis's reaction is a common one. People learn of new ideas in their businesses or professions, sense that they might easily have made the breakthrough themselves, quietly envy the other person for being lucky, and then continue in their customary unimaginative way, never realizing that luck can be created.

What could Dennis have done? After asking why he didn't think of the idea first, he could have asked, How might I extend the idea? What other creative applications are possible? Had he asked, he might have thought of grocery bags, truck posters, soda bottles, and the paychecks of state and federal employees. Each of these places, in fact, was subsequently used for ads after milk carton ads first appeared.

You can leapfrog others' achievements too, not only at work but at home as well. Take a new recipe, for example, and ask how you can modify it to suit your taste or dietary restrictions. Or take an idea for decorating your living room or rearranging your study or workshop— home improvement magazines are filled with original ideas that don't quite fit your situation—and decide how you can apply it to your needs.

Good-Habit Builder

The next time you encounter a good idea and find your-self saying, "I wish I had thought of that," ask yourself, "What other creative applications of this idea are possible?" and "How can I modify the idea to make it fit my special requirements?" Then put your ideas to work for you.

Tap Other People's Experience

When you begin to develop and use your creativity, you may become excessively self-reliant. In other words, your focus on finding and examining and solving problems may lead you to ignore other people's experience. This, of course, is unwise. Other people's experience can spare you costly and time-consuming mistakes and provide helpful insights. This is particularly true of the experience of researchers and other experts.

Does consulting others imply dependence? Not at all. It merely means reopening your mind, seeking greater understanding, becoming more interested in the world around you. Wearing eyeglasses will help you see more clearly; wearing a hearing aid will improve your hearing. Neither requires you to *approve* what you see or hear. Similarly, expanding your knowledge and understanding doesn't mean endorsing every idea you encounter. It just gives you a better basis for deciding what ideas are best.

Whenever you are dealing with a problem, think of as many sources of information as you can. Consider knowledgeable friends and acquaintances, as well as experts you don't know personally.

To find helpful reading material, including research studies, consult the reference librarian in your local library. Most libraries are part of an interlibrary loan system, so you will have access not just to thousands but to millions of titles.

Next, consider the expert opinion available locally. A

call to the appropriate county or state professional organization (for law, the bar association; for medicine, the medical association; and so on) will give you the name of an appropriate person to consult about the specific problem you are working on. A glance at the telephone company's Yellow Pages will suggest many possibilities. For example, if the problem concerns remodeling your home, you'll find architects, structural engineers, home builders, carpenters, general contractors, interior decorators, plumbers, electricians, and home improvement consultants.

Good-Habit Builder

Select a problem you are currently facing at work or in your personal life. Identify the best available sources of information concerning this problem and consult them. Incorporate their ideas with your own.

Anticipate Opposition

It's natural to reason, "If I have a good idea and take care to eliminate any flaws in it, it will surely find acceptance." Natural, but naive. No matter how worthwhile your idea may be, there will always be individuals who will dismiss it as worthless or attack it as harmful. Some people, unfortunately, take a skeet-shooting approach to life; they let other people toss up ideas, and they shoot them down. Since they never propose an idea, they never run the risk of rejection. And they enjoy the feeling of power and importance they get from criticizing the ideas of others.

These people are seldom in the majority, but their negativism can persuade other, more fair-minded people to join them in rejecting your idea. The more creative your idea is, the more susceptible people are to such persuasion. The progression *new* equals *radical* equals *unacceptable* makes a powerful argument in such cases.

To spare yourself disappointment and give your ideas a better chance of success, anticipate opposition and plan how you will neutralize it. After you have examined your idea critically, overcome imperfections and complications, and are ready to present it for other people's approval, ask yourself:

> Which individuals are likely to oppose this idea? What is the basis of their opposition likely to be? Is it possible that they will hide their real reasons? If so, what reasons will they state? (If you know the people involved, you will usually be able to answer these questions. If you don't know them, brainstorm with someone whose judgment you trust and identify probable lines of opposition.)

> How can I best respond to these criticisms? What data, including statistics, should I be prepared to offer? What explanations and/or arguments will be most effective? (Since there's little point in trying to change the minds of the skeet shooters, build your case to appeal to the fair-minded.)

If you aren't sure whether the person opposing your idea is an honest critic or a skeet shooter, ask for help in solving the problem or resolving the issue in question. If you don't get an answer, chances are he or she is a skeet shooter.

Good-Habit Builder

Select an idea you have that requires the acceptance of other people: perhaps a proposal at work or a plan for community action. Decide which individuals in the group you wish to persuade might oppose the idea and the specific objections they might raise. Evaluate each of these objections and plan your response to it. (If any objection points to a real flaw in your idea, revise your idea.)

6

Habits
for Sound Reasoning

Sound reasoning is the counterpart to creative thinking. Often called critical thinking, it is the evaluative side of the thought process and a crucial skill in everyday living. Virtually every challenge that confronts us demands that we evaluate ideas, our own as well as other people's. Unfortunately, since schools and colleges offer little or no training in sound reasoning, considerable confusion exists about it.

It is fashionable today to believe that all reasoning is equally sound. A false sense of democracy has converted "All men are created equal" into "All opinions are created equal." A false sense of tolerance has converted "Everyone has a right to an opinion" to "Everyone's opinion is right." Everyday experience demonstrates the foolishness of these notions.

"This stranger is well dressed and courteous, so I have nothing to fear in accepting a ride from him" is not sound reasoning. Neither are "If I ignore this sharp pain, it will surely go away," "I am a strong-willed person, so I can experiment with drugs without fear of addiction," and "Buying one lottery ticket is risky, but if I take all my savings and buy five thousand tickets, I've got an excellent chance of winning." People who think this way seldom escape the experience without paying a heavy price.

Among the most powerful temptations confronting us when we reason are the following:

> The temptation to accept what other people say un-questioningly (whether we embrace truth or error becomes in this case a matter of luck, and, given the myriad varieties of nonsense that abound today, the odds are against us)
>
> The temptation to think wishfully rather than logically
>
> The temptation to seek out ideas that flatter our point of view or encourage us to continue behaving as we wish to behave
>
> The temptation to act mindlessly and then attempt to justify our behavior

Good reasoning habits safeguard us against these and other errors that threaten our happiness and well-being.

Allow for Distortion

High school reunions are usually a lot of fun: people smiling, shaking hands, embracing, and recalling all the exciting times they shared. "Remember the prank we played on the principal?" "And what about our junior prom?" "Yes, and that hayride when Ed fell off the wagon?" An outsider, such as the wife or husband you met after you graduated, could easily be made envious and think, I wish I had gone to that school. What won-derful, happy times these people had!

It's puzzling to compare such recollections with what social scientists tell us about the teenage years. They are reportedly a time of great apprehension, fear, anxiety, and self-doubt. Teenagers worry about themselves and others' perception of them. "Am I too tall (short), too fat (skinny)? Are my feet too big (small)? Is my face . . . hair

... voice ... outfit ... ?" They agonize over whether people are laughing at them, whether they are considered nerds or freaks. And often their suffering has a basis in reality, when they are rejected by a sorority or a fraternity, fail to make the team or the cheerleading squad, are scorned by someone they admire, or forsaken by a sweetheart.

In light of this, we might expect the atmosphere at a high school reunion to be funerary. That it is not illustrates what research on remembering has long revealed: Memory is often distorted by attitude. In other words, we often remember events not as they were but as it now pleases us to *think* they were. Because this process is usually unconscious, we may be convinced we are recalling precisely what happened, when in fact we are selecting and rejecting details to fit our present attitude.

To compound the problem, our perception of present events is subject to a similar distortion. Contrary to popular opinion, eyewitness testimony is notoriously unreliable. Law school professors often demonstrate this to skeptical students by staging an unannounced dramatic confrontation in class. Several actors will begin shouting at one another, one will throw a wild punch, another will brandish a pistol, and so on. Then the professor will stop the drama, excuse the actors, and ask the class to write down an exact account of what they saw.

Their accounts, in many cases, are divergent. Some will have missed part of the action, others will get the sequence wrong. And at least a few will have seen their preconceptions rather than reality. For example, if the punching and gun brandishing were done by white students against a passive black student, some students still may remember the black student as the aggressor.

What does all this mean for us? Are we necessarily mired in subjective bias? Do we always see distortedly? Is it never possible for us to free ourselves from such errors? No. This simply means that we should acknowl-

edge the danger of distortion in our perception and remembering and make a special effort to see and recall
accurately. Further, it means we should make al-
lowances for distortion; whenever someone disputes our
version of what happened, we should be willing to consider the possibility that we were mistaken, at least in
part.

Good-Habit Builder

Monitor your perception and remembering. Take note
of matters about which you differ with others. Ask
yourself how your present attitude might be affecting
your memory and how bias might be coloring your
perception.

Understand Before Judging

A man begins speaking, and you realize that his view
opposes yours. You immediately begin thinking of how
you will answer him. A few minutes later, when he has
finished speaking, you are very clear about what you are
going to say, but you haven't the faintest notion of what
he said after his first sentence.

Sound familiar? Most of us react this way from time to
time. For some people, however, it's a characteristic response to those they disagree with. They not only judge
before understanding, they judge *instead of* understanding. And they do it in reading as well as in listening. The
moment they encounter a line that doesn't match their
thinking, their mind turns inward to rebuttal as their
eyes proceed vacantly down the page.

The first thing to be said of this habit is that it's unfair
to other people. Common courtesy, not to mention the
Golden Rule, demands more of us. To consider ourselves
above careful listening and reading is a sin of pride. Judging before understanding is the root form of prejudice

(prejudging). The proper time to judge someone's ideas is only after we have made the effort to understand them.

Judging before understanding is also foolish. The first sentence or group of sentences is seldom the measure of an entire speech or article. Most presentations are a mixture of good, fair, and poor ideas, and the precise proportions are not immediately evident. (Some may seem good or bad at first but, on closer examination, prove the reverse.) Only by an earnest effort to grasp all the ideas can we responsibly sort them out, embrace the good, and reject the bad.

Some people would object that this advice is unacceptable where matters of religious conviction are involved. Then, they argue, we should in effect say "Begone, Satan" as soon as we hear error expressed and immediately close our eyes and ears to avoid being led astray. They ignore the fact that error and truth are not so easily distinguishable at first encounter. Jesus admonished us, "Beware of false prophets, who come to you in sheep's clothing but inwardly are ravenous wolves" (Matt. 7:15). The task of distinguishing the genuine sheep from the wolf in disguise is too difficult, in most cases, to be done without careful thought.

The person we are tempted to close our minds to today may not be the ravenous wolf at all. The one we listened to so attentively yesterday may have been. The only way to separate them is to listen well and weigh carefully. In spiritual as in secular matters, impulsive reactions are not an asset but a liability.

Good-Habit Builder

Be alert today for occasions when you are listening to someone, or reading something, you disagree with. Resist the temptation to formulate a response instead of listening. Make a special effort to understand before judging.

Evaluate Information Sources

"It ain't what a man doesn't know that makes him a fool," Josh Billings observed, "but what he does know that ain't so." This idea is food for thought in the age of the information explosion.

We are bombarded by reports. TV news is broadcast around the clock. Newspapers and news magazines surround us. Talk shows spew forth a constant barrage of opinions. Supermarket publications trumpet the latest details of UFOs and the escapades of movie stars. It would be helpful if fact were neatly separated from interpretation, speculation, assumption, and guesswork (printed, for example, in a different color ink or accompanied by different musical tones).

Alas, we're not so fortunate. Fact and fiction, good and bad interpretation, responsible speculation and foolish fantasizing, sense and nonsense—all are intermingled. And the mixture appears so official, so believable. In our desire to be informed, we had best be wary of misinformation.

Even conscientious reporting is subject to error. For one thing, the reporter often arrives at the scene of some newsworthy event after it happens and may be barred from entering the exact area where it occurred. What happened must be pieced together from official statements, and the comments of people who witnessed the event. There may be no actual witnesses, and even if there are, their ranks will have been swelled by curiosity seekers. The reporter will more likely get comments from people who heard someone else in the crowd say what he thought another person who spoke to a witness believed she said . . . a rather unreliable mix.

Even if the event was announced in advance, as in the case of a politician's speech or a protest group's news conference, the report may be inaccurate. Reporters with strong feelings about the subject may slant their stories, depending on whether they agree or disagree with what is said. For example, a reporter who agrees may select only the most reasonable parts of the statement for the story. On the other hand, a reporter who disagrees may focus on one or two inflammatory or excessive statements. None of these flaws need be intentional. They may occur without the reporter's awareness—a case of bias imperceptibly controlling the judgment of what was significant.

A case in point occurred in a *Newsweek* article on the controversy over public funding of such art as Andres Serrano's photograph "Piss Christ" (a crucifix in a bucket of urine). Throughout the article, the author disparaged those who object to such funding with terms such as "morals squad," "artbusters," "righter-than-thou," "inflammatory," and "stiff-necked moralists." However, in describing the creators of these works and their supporters, he used almost exclusively favorable or neutral terms. The message, intentionally or not, was that anyone who opposed public funding of such art is a self-righteous fool.[5]

The reporter may, of course, recognize and control his or her bias and produce an eminently fair account of what happened, only to have the story altered by an editor who responds to the pressure of media competition by sensationalizing the news. The headline alone can accomplish this by creating impressions the story does not justify.

In situations where the news is accompanied by commentary, as it is on editorial pages and TV news analysis programs, the chances of error are multiplied. For here the emphasis is on assessing the meaning and significance of the news item, a considerably more difficult task.

It makes good sense to raise pointed questions about

the sources from which you receive your information. The following questions are among the most important.

How Reliable Is the Source?

All authors and TV and radio newspeople are *not* equally reputable. Some are known for their integrity and accuracy in reporting; others are careless and given to sensationalizing events. Before accepting any information, ask yourself, "Just how reliable is this source?"

How Well Documented Is the Report?

First-hand observation is less likely to be flawed than a second- or third-hand report. But even eyewitness testimony can be undermined by the drama of a situation and the strong emotion it arouses. So develop the habit of asking, "Were the witnesses trained observers? Could any circumstances—rain, fog, dark of night, the distance involved, the brevity of the incident, or their state of mind—have affected their perception?"

How Qualified Are the Commentators?

More often than not, factual information is combined with interpretation or judgment. It is up to the reader or viewer to separate the two and, in the case of interpretation or judgment, to appraise the qualifications of the commentator. It's not uncommon for talk-show hosts and their celebrity guests to parade their views on religion, philosophy, world politics, and other subjects in which they lack the slightest expertise. Moreover, they will often state their uninformed opinions as if they were facts. Keep in mind that having a right to an opinion does not make that opinion right, and keep asking yourself, "What competency, if any, do these people have in the matters they are discussing?"

Good-Habit Builder

For the next few days when you read newspapers and magazines or watch TV news and talk shows, inquire about the reliability of sources, the quality of the documentation, and the qualifications of the commentators.

Avoid Errors of Perception

Errors of perception are not specific mistakes made while reasoning about a particular matter. They are, rather, faulty perspectives that prevent us from observing any situation accurately. The following five errors are among the most serious.

"Mine is better." It's natural for little children to think that their toys, pets, blankets, and daddies and mommies are better than other people's. In time most of us develop a more mature perspective. But some people retain that view and extend it to their opinions and actions. They really believe that "Whatever I think and do is right and whatever opposes my way is wrong." This perspective prevents them from being fair-minded and objective. They will not consider other views; their minds are made up in advance.

Selective perception. This consists of seeing whatever supports our preconceived notions and ignoring whatever does not. A man who believes Jews are greedy will close his eyes to a dozen examples of Jewish philanthropy and focus on one case that supports his view. I know a woman who is forever complaining that welfare is ruining our nation, yet she thought nothing of using her political influence to get her son a no-show government job while he was attending law school. By any reasonable measure, her son and the children of a number of her friends were also welfare recipients, but she conveniently avoided such comparisons.

Pretending to know. This error usually results from fear of being considered ignorant. It not only stifles our natural curiosity but also prevents us from inquiring. Since in complex matters the quality of our reasoning is affected by our level of knowledge, pretending to know is a serious impediment to sound judgment.

Resistance to change. A sensible attitude toward change is, "If a new idea or new way of doing something proves to be better than the old, I will embrace it." But many people resist all change, either because they are afraid that they will be unable to adjust to the new or because they believe that old ways are always better. The latter view doesn't allow for the fact that human inventions, like humans themselves, are imperfect and therefore can always be improved. Resistance to change blocks honest judgment.

Either/or thinking. This error consists of believing that there is no middle ground in controversial issues. Many people take an either/or position on the evolution vs. creationism issue, arguing that the two are incompatible. In fact, they are compatible; many Christians accept evolution as part of God's plan of creation. Similarly, the view that prison must be either a place of punishment or of rehabilitation is erroneous; it can be both. And the popular idea that everyone must be either "right-brained" or "left-brained" is considered by most experts as half-brained. In other words, their research documents that, in normal people, the two hemispheres of the brain are profoundly integrated.[6]

Good-Habit Builder

Monitor your thinking for errors of perspective. Note occasions when you are guilty of "mine is better" thinking, selective perception, pretending to know, resistance to change, or either/or thinking. Resolve to overcome any errors you find.

Avoid Errors of Judgment

Errors of judgment are flaws in reasoning. They occur when we evaluate information, interpret it, and draw conclusions about it. Among the most serious of these errors are the following.

Illogical conclusion. A conclusion is illogical if it does not follow from the evidence. In situations where there are two or more possible conclusions and the evidence does not point clearly to one, we should refrain from deciding until we have more evidence. "I know he drinks a lot and can't hold a job, but after we're married he'll change" is illogical because it embraces one possibility ("he'll change") and ignores the opposing one ("he won't change") for no apparent reason other than wishful thinking. "If we reduce the taxes of the rich, the rich will create more jobs for the poor" is illogical because it is equally possible that the rich will pocket the savings and turn their backs on the poor.

Double standard. This error consists of being generous in our assessments of ourselves and those we like and ungenerous in our assessments of others. For example, many people expect others to repay their debts promptly but take forever to repay their own creditors. And many demand courtesy, punctuality, and consideration from others but feel no compunction about denying them equal treatment.

When judging ideas, they employ the same double standard, overlooking the flaws in views compatible with their own and magnifying the flaws in opposing views. Even the words they use to describe others will often reflect their double standard. Their friends are thrifty;

their enemies, stingy. People they like are "given to ex-
aggeration"; those they dislike are congenital liars. If
such people are white and prejudiced they will see a
black person on drugs as a drug addict but a white person as "substance dependent." A black person who can't
read and write will be illiterate, whereas a white person
will have a "learning disability."

Using a double standard is not only intellectually dishonest and unfair; it is also a form of hypocrisy.

Overgeneralization. Generalizations classify people,
places, institutions, and ideas according to their common
elements. When we say that professional bodybuilders
are heavily muscled, four-cylinder cars get better mile-
age than eight-cylinder cars, feminists are concerned
about women's rights, and fundamentalist Christians ad-
vocate literal interpretation of the Bible, we are general-
izing. Moreover, each of these generalizations is fair and
accurate.

*Over*generalization, as the term implies, is excessive.
It violates fairness and accuracy by ignoring individual
differences in matters where such differences are both
common and numerous. Here are some examples of
overgeneralization: "Feminists hate men," "City dwell-
ers are less friendly than suburbanites," "Educated people lack common sense," and "College athletes do
poorly in their studies." ("Athletes," remember, covers
not just football and basketball players but swimmers,
golfers, track and field competitors, and bowlers, among
others.)

Many overgeneralizations are the result of careless
thinking: more specifically, saying or implying *all* where
only *some* or *many* is justified. Some, however, are emo-
tionally charged and irrationally maintained. These are
known as "stereotypes" and are more difficult to overcome. The most common ones are racial, religious, sexual, and ethnic, and they may be either positive or

negative. There are, for example, stereotypes of blacks, Hispanics, Jews, the clergy, homosexuals, feminists, male chauvinists, and motherhood.

Hasty conclusion. A hasty conclusion is a premature judgment. It occurs when two or more conclusions are possible and the available evidence does not clearly favor any one of them, yet we seize either the first one that we think of or the one that fits our mood at the moment. If we notice that a certain man puts nothing in the collection plate on Sunday, we may hastily conclude that he is refusing to support the church. But other conclusions are possible: He may have forgotten his envelope, or he may mail in his offering, or he may give monthly instead of weekly.

Even professionals can commit this error. For example, at least one study revealed that some physicians make diagnoses on the very first symptom the patient presents and ignore those presented later. And many social scientists, observing that humans have much in common with animals, have concluded that humans are "nothing but animals." (The even more remarkable differences between humans and animals cannot reasonably be ignored.)

Oversimplification. It is acceptable to simplify a complex reality in order to understand it or communicate it to others. Teachers do it all the time. *Over*simplifying, however, is never acceptable because it denies complexity and distorts reality. A common objection to public assistance for the poor and needy is, "Give people a handout and you make bums of them." This is an oversimplification. Not that it's totally false; lazy, irresponsible people undoubtedly are made more so by public assistance. But hardworking, responsible people who are victimized by serious illness or other misfortune are surely not corrupted.

Good-Habit Builder

Think of a situation when you have been guilty of one or more of these errors of judgment: illogical conclusion, double standard, overgeneralization, hasty conclusion, oversimplification. In each case, consider how you could have avoided the error.

Avoid Errors of Reaction

Errors of reaction usually occur after we make up our minds about an issue and express our view and someone challenges us. They are defensive responses that preserve our self-image and provide an excuse to reject the challenge and go on believing as we wish. The most common errors of reaction are the following four.

Explaining Away. This error consists of rationalizing or making excuses to justify rejecting unpleasant truths. If a wife chastises her husband for cashing a check that was sent to him in error, he may say, "This makes up for all the times I've been overcharged in stores." If he scolds her for stuffing hotel towels into her suitcase, she may respond, "They expect guests to take towels; the room rate includes a built-in cost to cover it." Both are guilty of explaining away.

Not long ago, a reader wrote the editor of a small northeast daily newspaper, expressing dissatisfaction with the frequent grammatical errors and confused expression in news reports and opinion columns. Since the reader cited numerous examples of such errors, we might think that the editor would have accepted the reproof and apologized for his staff. Instead, he offered the following pathetic excuses: The schools are at fault for not teaching writing effectively, modern electronic communication makes such mistakes inevitable, and his staff places higher priority on news gathering than on proofreading. The editor's attempt to explain away the reader's legitimate criticism surely fooled no one but himself.

Shifting the burden of proof. The term "burden of proof" means the responsibility for supporting our assertions. Whoever makes an assertion should be ready to support it, if asked to. If you say, "Negative political campaigning is a greater problem today than in the past," it's fair for someone who is skeptical or disagrees to ask, "What leads you to that conclusion?" If you respond, "That's what I think, prove me wrong if you can," you are being intellectually dishonest in shifting the burden of proof. (You, of course, have the same right to ask others to support *their* assertions.)

Attacking the person. There are times when it is appropriate to focus on someone's character; for example, when the subject of discussion is whether a political candidate is guilty of an ethical offense. Attacking the person is an error when it unreasonably diverts attention from the issue at hand. This error usually occurs when someone has pointed out a flaw in our thinking and we are feeling embarrassed. Let's say Marge has been arguing that once someone has been convicted of a capital crime, execution should be carried out immediately. Sally says, "That would deny people the right of appeal. In some cases, the appeal process reveals that crucial evidence has been suppressed and the convicted person is really innocent." Marge's pride prevents her from saying, "That's an excellent point. I didn't consider such cases"; instead she launches into an attack on Sally. "You're always looking for chances to pick on me. I remember the time . . . " This is attacking the person.

Irrational appeals. The most common irrational appeals are to authority ("We have no business questioning the experts"), tradition ("We mustn't change what is long established"), common practice ("Everyone does it"), fear ("Awful things could happen"), and moderation ("Let's compromise so as not to offend anyone"). There is nothing inherently wrong with these appeals. Each of them is legitimate in many situations. It is only when they are used to short-circuit thought and excite the emotions that they are improper.

Good-Habit Builder

Think of situations in which you have explained away, shifted the burden of proof, attacked the person, or made irrational appeals. In each case, consider how you could have avoided the error.

Examine Your Assumptions

Assuming is taking something for granted. Unlike reasoning, it is an unconscious process, a kind of mental arithmetic that we are usually unaware of. Some assumptions are warranted; for example, we are justified in assuming that if our car is in good condition, it will start tomorrow morning. (Even if it doesn't start, our assumption was still reasonable under the circumstances.) Other assumptions are unwarranted; for example, the assumption that if we've never had an accident speeding on icy roads, we never will have one, or that, when things don't go our way, we have a right to be outraged and punish others.

Since we can take too much for granted in any situation and under any set of circumstances, it is impossible to list all the unwarranted assumptions we should avoid. Nevertheless, the following ones tend to recur in a variety of forms.

Assuming that your point of view is an unassailable truth (or the only point of view). Since you are human and capable of error, your point of view may be mistaken.

Assuming that conviction equals proof. It is possible to believe something with every fiber of your being and have it be wrong.

Assuming that familiar arguments are necessarily true. What we have heard first or most frequently will seem true, but there is no assurance that we always hear the truth first.

Assuming that the majority view is correct. Majorities are often wrong. (In ancient times, the majority approved infanticide; more recently, slavery.)

Assuming that the way things are is the way they should be. Many beneficial, fair, and moral practices have become established in tradition, but so have many harmful, unfair, and immoral practices.

Assuming that eyewitness testimony is necessarily accurate. As explained earlier in this chapter, in discussing evaluation, it is often quite unreliable.

Assuming that, if something went wrong, someone must be at fault. Things sometimes go wrong despite the best efforts of those involved.

Good-Habit Builder

Monitor your thinking for assumptions. Remember that they are not conscious reasoning but unconscious taking-for-granted, so you will have to look for subtle clues that you are assuming. Evaluate each assumption to decide whether it is warranted.

Make Important Distinctions

One of the most serious obstacles to sound reasoning is the tendency to confuse things that are in some ways alike but have subtle but significant differences. Making important distinctions means noticing those differences. It would be impossible to list all the important distinctions; their form often changes with the situation. (For example, the distinction between the words *seldom* and *never* is essentially the same as that between *often* and *always*, yet the implications of the two sets are diametrically opposite.) The following distinctions are important in a variety of circumstances.

The distinction between the person and the idea. If we confuse the person with the idea, we will be tempted to accept the ideas of people we admire and reject the ideas of those we dislike. But admirable people can err, and unlikable, even disreputable people are capable of insight. Judge ideas on their own merits, irrespective of their proponents.

The distinction between fact and interpretation. A fact is something that can be known with certainty, something objectively verifiable or demonstrable. An interpretation is a judgment about meaning or significance. Confusing the two can lead to uncritical acceptance of statements that ought to be weighed and evaluated.

The distinction between assertion and evidence. Saying something is so does not make it so, no matter how great the conviction or the eloquence of the spokesperson. Neither does repeating the idea numerous times in different words. Careful thinkers look beyond assertions to the evidence supporting them.

The distinction between informed and uninformed opinions. Everyone is free to form an opinion, but that doesn't mean every opinion is right. There is no guarantee that informed or expert opinion will always be right, but it is much more reliable than uninformed opinion. Careful thinkers distinguish between the two and seek out informed opinion.

The distinction between thought and feeling. The problem is not that feeling is bad—it isn't—but that it is capricious and therefore shouldn't be trusted before we think about it and evaluate it. Distinguishing between thought and feeling will help you avoid judging on first impressions and other impulsive reactions.

The distinction between familiarity and validity. Confusing familiarity with validity leads us to accept ideas just because we have heard them before, and that is unreasonable. We hear good ideas and bad, wisdom and absurdity, all the time. In any given case, it may be the unfamiliar idea that deserves our endorsement.

Good-Habit Builder

Think of occasions when you failed to make important distinctions. Decide how you would have thought, spoken, or acted if you had made the distinctions. Try to identify future situations in which it will be important to make them.

Acknowledge Controversy

A controversy is a profound difference of opinion over an important issue. In virtually every controversy, each side of the dispute can claim the support of some intelligent, informed people because each side has some merit. This doesn't mean that each side is 50 percent correct; the odds are heavily against this possibility, as they are against the possibility of one side being totally right and the other entirely wrong. The ratio may be 60:40, 75:25, or 99:1.

One reason so many controversial issues remain unresolved for decades or longer is that most people refuse to see them as controversial. In other words, their attitude is: "My view is 100 percent correct, and only a fool would disagree." Not surprisingly, this attitude closes their minds and often prompts the other side to intransigence.

Both liberals and conservatives are guilty of pretending that the other view has no merit and of focusing exclusively on finding flaws in the other side's arguments, thus ensuring that neither side will see its own. For example, when conservatives attacked the homoerotic art of Robert Mapplethorpe and the music of the rap music group 2 Live Crew (discussed in chapter 3), liberals criticized them for reacting on the basis of hearsay. "They ought at least to have the decency and fairness to see the art or hear the music before they condemn it."

But at the very moment they uttered those words, most of those liberals were committing *the very error they were protesting:* defending things they hadn't seen or heard. (We can be sure of this because throughout most of the furor the media refused to describe the paintings or print the song lyrics.)

How can you be sure you are really acknowledging the controversies you deal with? By following these guidelines.

Remind yourself of the possibility that neither side of a controversial issue possesses the total truth. To get that truth, you may have to combine the insights of the two sides.

Don't regard all your views as convictions. Your interpretation of the meaning of one of Jesus' parables, for example, does not deserve the same unswerving allegiance as your belief in God or in the divinity of Jesus.

Seek out dissenting views. Listen to the views of those on the other side of the issue. Weigh them fairly, noting insights as well as errors, and incorporate the insights with your own ideas.

Have the courage to question your own ideas. This is not the same as being a skeptic. Skeptics doubt systematically because they deny truth. Careful thinkers ask tough questions about all ideas because they affirm the truth and want their thinking to reflect it.

Delay reacting when you are impulsive. The exchange of ideas on controversial issues can make us all emotional, too much so, in many cases, for reason to prevail. Whenever necessary, set the issue aside and return to it when you can address it calmly and fairly.

Good-Habit Builder

List some views you feel strongly about. Don't limit yourself to a single subject; include, for example, your views on financial investments, employer-employee relations, parenting, education, and criminal justice. Then, over the next week or two, seek out some knowledgeable people who disagree with one of your views. If you know such people personally, fine: if not, visit the library. Listen to (or read) their ideas carefully and fairmindedly. Then decide whether some modification of your original idea is appropriate.

Check Your Evidence

How are you at balancing your checkbook? Unless you are an unusual person, your performance falls somewhat short of perfection. You may be diligent about entering the information for each check as you write it, perform your arithmetic with reasonable care, and feel quite confident that your checkbook is error-free. But when the bank statement comes, you realize that someone has erred, and usually it's not the bank.

Reasoning works much the same way. We are constantly forming conclusions: about career matters; about the motivations and intentions of people; about social problems and proposals for solving them; about the quality of service provided by doctors, lawyers, teachers, elected officials; about religious and philosophical questions; about marital relations and parenting; about local, national, and international issues. Unfortunately, we don't get a statement from the world each month that prods us to balance our conclusion book. So the errors we make tend to remain undetected and frequently are compounded.

To minimize your errors in reasoning, develop the habit of checking your evidence. Whenever you find yourself reaching a conclusion, challenge yourself in the following manner. (It's best to raise these questions before you express your judgment to anyone. Once you do so, your ego will become involved and fear of losing face will make it more difficult to change your mind.)

"OK, this is the conclusion that seems right to me. But what evidence am I basing it on? What have I seen or heard or read that supports it? What are some other possible conclusions? Does the evidence fit one of them better than the one I've tentatively chosen? Is it possible that the evidence available at this time is inconclusive?"

Good-Habit Builder

For the next twenty-four hours remain alert to the conclusions you make. Before you express them to others, challenge each one by asking yourself (1) what other conclusions are *possible*, (2) what evidence do I have for choosing my conclusion over the others, and (3) is that evidence sufficient? Revise your conclusions as necessary.

Reopen Closed Issues

In the late 1980s a college senior discovered a mathematical error in Isaac Newton's famous *Mathematical Principles of Natural Philosophy*. Scholars were astounded. The student's professor said he had always wondered why he couldn't get his own calculations to match Newton's. The error had gone undetected for three hundred years. Imagine how many mathematicians, distinguished professors, and Nobel prize winners had stared at that error and failed to see it!

Is such an oversight difficult to understand? Not really. Although this case is more dramatic than most, human history is filled with similar examples. For thousands of years the earth was considered the center of the universe. For centuries the heart, rather than the brain, was considered the center of consciousness, and the severe chest pain that signals a heart attack was diagnosed as "acute indigestion."

Once an issue has been settled to society's satisfaction, people tend to regard it as closed, and history must await the advent of someone curious or bold enough to reopen the matter. In the case of Newton's error, his towering position in the history of science was enough to make others regard him as infallible. And so it took three hundred years for someone to think, "Perhaps Newton made an error."

A similar tendency exists in each of us. Once we have personally made up our minds about an issue, we treat it as settled. And at that moment our ego becomes involved, and ever afterward we think, "I couldn't have made a mistake," or, "If I'm wrong I'll be embarrassed, so I'll refuse to consider the possibility."

Good sense demands that we acknowledge that we may be wrong; love of truth demands that we carry our opinions lightly. This doesn't mean we should lack conviction or question our own views every time we encounter someone with a different idea. It means only that we should be ready to reconsider our view of any issue when we encounter evidence that calls it into question. We cannot lose with this approach. If our original view withstands scrutiny, we can embrace it with even greater conviction. If it proves to be mistaken, we will profit from revising it.

Good-Habit Builder

The next time you read or hear evidence that calls one of your viewpoints into question, resist the urge to dismiss that evidence. Instead, rethink your position. If you fear that such openness to other ideas represents abandonment of your convictions, remind yourself that a worthy conviction will survive close examination.

7

Habits
for Effective
Communication

There is a widely accepted belief that the only skills that matter for business and professional people are those pertaining directly to their fields. Students majoring in engineering, mathematics, chemistry, physics, accounting, management, and many other fields often complain about having to take courses in speaking and writing. They believe technical expertise is all they need for success in life. This belief is mistaken.

Communication is so important, in fact, that large corporations spend most of their $35 billion annual employee training budget on it. Employees in responsible positions are expected to write memorandums, letters, and reports and speak understandably with fellow employees. The demand for specialization has also created a need for team problem solving, which necessitates regular communication with men and women from different areas of expertise. And many business and professional people regularly speak on the telephone or in person with suppliers, distributors, government agency personnel, community leaders, customers, and representatives of the media.

When employees lack the skills of effective communication, the result can be costly. Poor communication causes misunderstanding, waste, inefficiency, and error, as well as loss of quality control, employee morale, and customer goodwill. That is why promotions and salary increases are usually reserved for men and women who demonstrate not only technical skills but also proficiency in writing and speaking.

Nor is communication any less important in our personal lives. Making a success of marriage and parenthood is largely a matter of communicating effectively with our spouses, children, and other relatives. Friendships, too, often stand or fall on the quality of the communication. It is not enough to feel empathy, understanding, support, love, and commitment; we must know how to express them to others.

All things considered, the investment of effort in developing the habits of effective communication is among the soundest we can make.

Study Effective Speakers

It's not necessary to be a professional critic to know that some speakers are more effective than others. One lecturer can hold an audience spellbound for hours while the next has people rushing for the exits in a matter of minutes. Most of us, most of the time, don't conduct any formal analysis of the speakers we listen to. We just react. We like a speaker or we don't, and that's that.

However, if we want to become better communicators ourselves, it's helpful to examine our reactions to other speakers. Exactly what makes us enjoy listening to this person? What specific qualities does he or she have that appeal to us? Conversely, what qualities make us react unfavorably? These are the questions to explore.

Public-speaking experts have identified a number of specific characteristics of effective speakers. Chief among them are the three that follow.

A well-organized, easy-to-follow message. The intro-duction gets the audience's attention, makes clear what the speech will be about, and establishes credibility and goodwill. In most cases it is no more than several sen-tences in length. The body consists of a central idea, together with adequate explanation and support (from four to seven supporting points is standard), logically arranged. The conclusion reinforces the central idea and, where appropriate, urges the audience to action. Wherever possible, visual aids are used to help the audi-ence understand and remember key points.

A strong and pleasant voice. Effective speakers speak loud enough to be heard throughout the room, but not so loud as to be distracting. Their pitch is neither too high nor too low and has sufficient inflection (variation) to fit the meaning of the words and emotion that under-lie them. Inflection can convey anger or pleasure, enthu-siasm or boredom, tenseness or relaxation.

Good speakers maintain a rate of delivery that is ap-propriate to the occasion, audience, and message and is sufficiently varied to create interest—somewhere be-tween 120 and 150 words a minute, on average. They build in pauses to create suspense and drama, as well as to allow the audience to grasp the full import of the idea. As Mark Twain observed, "The right word may be effective, but no word was ever as effective as a rightly timed pause."

Variety governs all the above elements. Effective speakers speed up and slow down, raise and lower their pitch, are louder and then softer, and build in pauses of various lengths, all in a way that conveys enthusiasm and thus stimulates interest.

Effective speakers also pronounce words correctly and enunciate (articulate) precisely. In addition, their tone (the attitude they convey) is appropriate to the occasion. In general, tone should suggest quiet confidence, friendliness, and approachability. A sarcastic, scolding, or know-it-all tone is never appropriate.

Positive nonverbal communication. Effective speakers look, as well as sound, professional. It is possible to dress too formally, but that is much less a problem, as a rule, than dressing too informally. A jacket and tie for a man or a conservative dress or suit for a woman are almost always appropriate. Good grooming is also essential. "I respect myself and my audience" should be the clear, though unstated, message.

Since an audience's evaluation begins from the moment the speaker rises to approach the podium to the moment he or she sits down at the close, every movement should convey confidence, seriousness of purpose, and self-control. Some effective speakers gesture a lot, others very little. In either case, gesturing should be natural and well timed to reinforce the verbal message.

Effective speakers make frequent eye contact with the audience, moving their eyes from person to person to include everyone, engaging them and commanding their attention. They take care to look at people's eyes, not over their heads or at some point on the back wall.

Though all three of the above characteristics are associated with public speaking, they apply to conversation and group discussion as well. However, these latter situations are informal, so expression is more spontaneous and alternates with listening.

One good way to appreciate the importance and the interplay of these characteristics is to analyze the speaking effectiveness of well-known people: elected officials such as George Bush, Ted Kennedy, Robert Dole, and Mario Cuomo; news analysts and commentators such as Ted Koppel, Mike Wallace, Hugh Downs, and Barbara Walters; talk-show hosts such as Oprah Winfrey and Phil Donahue; and religious leaders such as Pat Robertson, Billy Graham, and Robert Schuller.

Don't limit your analysis to living speakers. Check your local library for videotapes or audiotapes of renowned speakers such as Winston Churchill, Franklin D. Roosevelt, John F. Kennedy, and Martin Luther King, Jr.

Good-Habit Builder

Choose a speaker who often appears on television, preferably on a program offering at least several minutes of organized, uninterrupted presentation—perhaps a government hearing, a press conference, or a sermon. (Avoid comedy routines, situation comedies, and game shows.) Tune in and study the person's presentation. For best results, videotape it so you can play it over and over and study it thoroughly. Decide what strengths and weaknesses the speaker has and how they affect overall performance and influence audience reaction.

Analyze Your Speaking Style

You can learn a great deal from analyzing other people's speaking styles, and this will deepen your understanding of the principles of good speaking. To improve your own speaking, however, you'll need to analyze it and find your strengths and weaknesses.

It's difficult to evaluate your style while you are speaking, so you're better off taping yourself and playing the tape back later. If you are a teacher or a salesperson, you'll be able to tape your presentations without others knowing. Even if you don't do any formal speaking, you have lots of opportunities for taping. These include telephone conversations, meetings at work, and family discussions. (In many cases, you will have an ethical obligation to let others know that you are taping them.)

One excellent way to analyze your speaking voice is to tape yourself doing a dramatic reading. To find an appropriate speech, visit your library and choose a book of famous speeches or consult *Vital Speeches of the Day*.

If you have never heard a tape of your voice before, be prepared for a surprise. Because we usually hear ourselves within our personal sound chamber, we seldom hear ourselves as others hear us. The voice you hear on tape is the voice others hear. Listen until the strangeness wears off. Then listen again analytically and rate yourself on the characteristics of effective speaking just discussed.

Good-Habit Builder

Tape yourself in conversation and then again in a more formal situation. Listen critically and identify your strengths and weaknesses.

Work on Your Weaknesses

Everyone has some weaknesses in speaking. One person may have a thin voice that is not easily heard. Another may tend to speak in a monotone. A third may not enunciate clearly. But there are few weaknesses that cannot be overcome, or at least compensated for, by diligent effort.

Practice is the key to success even for those blessed with unusually good voices. Even though actor E. G. Marshall had a strong voice to begin with, he nevertheless devoted years to improving it, particularly by practicing speaking slowly and paying careful attention to vowels. As a young man, Richard Burton went up to a mountaintop in his native Wales and shouted lines from Shakespeare into the wind to make his already powerful voice even stronger.

Here are the most common weaknesses in speaking and suggestions for overcoming them.

Volume too loud or too soft. Some people scream and others speak in a near whisper. Sometimes the cause of this problem is a hearing deficiency they are unaware of. If you find you speak very loud or soft, you may wish to have your hearing checked. If it is normal, just make a conscious effort to adjust the volume down or up.

Speaking rate too fast or slow. The effects of these weaknesses are, respectively, that your listeners will lose track of your ideas or they will grow bored. Play back a tape of yourself speaking and measure your rate. If it averages much more than 150 words per minute, practice speaking more slowly; if much less than 120 words a minute, practice speaking faster. (The key word in the previous sentence is "averages." Variations in speed are both natural and desirable.)

Annoying voice characteristics. If your voice is shrill, raspy, whiny, or has a pronounced nasal quality, it is likely to detract from your speaking effectiveness. Listen to a tape of your voice and determine whether you have such a quality. If you do, and if you can rule out a nose or throat condition as the cause, practice speaking in front of a mirror and concentrate on overcoming the offensive quality.

Too little inflection. People who speak in a monotone usually find themselves talking in other people's sleep. One way to overcome this problem in public speaking is to choose topics you feel strongly about. Enthusiasm will add excitement and variety to your delivery. Also, try speaking animatedly or doing dramatic readings, at first in front of a mirror and then in front of others. If this will embarrass you, read aloud, with exaggerated feeling, to a child.

Running sentences together. Punctuation is as important in speaking as in writing; it helps the listener grasp your meaning. Punctuation in speaking, of course, is heard, rather than seen, and is represented by pauses (commas) and brief stops (periods). If you tend to run your sentences together, practice reading letters, articles, or stories aloud and pausing or stopping to signal the punctuation.

Audible pauses. Audible pauses take the form of "um," "uh," and "ah." Used frequently, they are among the most aggravating of speech flaws. Many speakers who have this problem are completely unaware of it, so the best way to detect it in your speaking is to tape yourself a number of times, in various speaking situations, and listen carefully for these sounds. Then, whenever you speak, remind yourself that pauses must be silent to be effective and make a conscious effort not to utter a sound when you use them.

Errors in pronunciation. These occur when syllables are inserted (*ath-a-lete* instead of *ath-lete*), omitted (*partic-lar* instead of *par-tic-u-lar*), formed incorrectly (*Feb-you-ary* for *Feb-ru-ary,*), or switched (*rev-e-lant* instead of *rel-e-vant*). When in doubt about the correct pronunciation of a word, consult a good dictionary. Here is a starter list of words frequently mispronounced: *arctic, larynx, library, recognize, theater, truth, ask, picture, nuclear, mischievous.*

Careless articulation. Unlike errors in pronunciation, this error occurs when you know the correct pronunciation but form word sounds sloppily; for example, saying *wit* for *with, didja* for *did you, oughta* for *ought to, gonna* for *going to, sposed* for *supposed, dunno* for *don't know, guvmint* for *government,* and *dem* for *them.* Demosthenes, the famous Greek orator, reportedly put small stones in his mouth to make himself speak ever more clearly. You may not want to go to this extreme (at least not without washing the stones), but you can practice enunciating word sounds with care.

Lack of feeling and animation in voice or manner. In public speaking this problem is often caused by reading the speech, rather than delivering it, and staring at the paper while doing so. The solution is to take key words, but not a prepared speech, to the podium. To develop a more animated style, practice reading poetry aloud. (Choose poetry that expresses feelings that match your own.) Or sing songs with great feeling in them. In either case, make your voice express the feeling and let your body movement and your gestures punctuate it. Do this often enough that you feel comfortable and natural being dramatic.

If you have a regional or a foreign accent, don't be concerned. Although an accent used to be considered a handicap to be overcome, most speech authorities today agree that it can actually be an asset. A woman in my church occasionally does a scripture reading. She obviously came to this country from Ireland because her brogue is still strong. But because her enunciation is impeccable, her accent does not detract from her delivery. Listening to her read is a pleasure rather than a chore. This is not only true of foreign accents but of regional ones, as well. If you have one, don't try to lose it. Just aim for clarity.

Good-Habit Builder

Monitor your speaking for these common weaknesses: volume too loud or soft, speaking rate too fast or slow, annoying voice characteristics, too little inflection, running sentences together, audible pauses, errors in pronunciation, careless articulation, and lack of feeling and animation in voice or manner. You may wish to enlist a friend or your spouse in making your self-assessment and in evaluating your progress.

Forget Yourself When Speaking in Public

Your name is called. The moment is here and you've dreaded it ever since you were asked to introduce the main speaker at the banquet. As you push back your chair, the same thoughts return for the thousandth time. Will I make a fool of myself? Will I pronounce the speaker's name correctly? Am I dressed right? Do I look as out of place as I feel? I'm going to look ridiculous up there, I know it. What if I forget what I'm going to say? Why did I agree to make the introduction? Oh, I wish it were over!

As you walk to the podium, your mouth is dry, your hands are wet, your knees are knocking, and your stomach is fluttering madly. And why not? You've just talked yourself into a state of anxiety.

Could you have avoided punishing yourself that way? Absolutely. Even the most accomplished speakers get nervous before they speak, sometimes to the point of feeling ill. But they have learned how to make nervousness an ally by transforming it into energy, dynamism.

The secret is to stop focusing on self. Look back at the number of times "I" is used in that first paragraph: eleven times. And for no good reason. The audience is not there to hear the introduction; they're tolerating that, and you, as a necessary preliminary to the speech they came to hear. As difficult as it may be to accept, you just aren't that important in this situation.

What, then, should you focus on, if not yourself? The speaker you are introducing, his or her interesting and impressive accomplishments, the significance of the topic on this occasion, the pleasure and value you antici-pate this message will give the audience, the positive things they are going to say later, at the reception. The moment you turn your thoughts away from yourself and onto these things, your nervousness will be under control.

But what should you focus on when you are not the introducer but the main speaker? Your message and your audience. If you have chosen a topic you are knowledgeable about and have a firm view on, and this should always be the case, think about how important your message is to your audience and how they will benefit from what you will say. Let these thoughts stimulate your commitment and enthusiasm for making the speech. Concentrate on carrying out your planned delivery and suppress all thoughts of self. (This same advice applies to informal speaking situations.)

It will also help to remind yourself that other people cannot see what is going on inside you unless you let them. Following the approaches explained here will ensure that others see you as calm and at ease even if you are experiencing some nervousness.

Good-Habit Builder

The next time you have to speak in public, formally or otherwise, combat nervousness by focusing on the subject and the audience. Don't be discouraged if thoughts about yourself intrude. Just refuse to indulge them.

Listen Intently

Listening is a vital skill. Lacking it, we are almost certain to be uninformed or misinformed. And yet listening is among the most neglected of skills today, for several reasons. One is the simple fact that the rate at which we can process information is about four times the average speaking rate. Unless the speaker is lively, we can easily fall victim to daydreaming.

Another reason for poor listening is an increase in

what Edmond Addeo and Robert Burger call "ego-speak," the habit of ignoring what other people are saying if it doesn't match our interests. A third reason is the habit of wondering about the speaker's motives instead of paying attention to what the speaker is saying. "His voice is rising, so he obviously feels strongly about what he's saying. But why should he be so upset with what happened? Maybe it's because . . . "

Yet another reason for poor listening is the habit of classifying the speaker. "She sounds like someone I've heard before. Who is it? Someone at work? Someone in my old neighborhood? I've got it—Betty Collins. She sounds just like Betty Collins." Or "He's talking like a conservative. I didn't ever peg him for a conservative. Maybe he's liberal about some issues but not about others. I wonder where he stands on . . . "

Finally, poor listening may be caused by the urge to respond to what is being said. The speaker, for example, may say, "Let me explain why I believe the Federal Communications Commission should ban wine and beer ads from television." If we disagree, we immediately cease listening and begin planning a rebuttal: "No, they shouldn't. There's nothing wrong with drinking in moderation. To prohibit a perfectly legal industry from advertising its products is an improper intrusion into the marketplace. . . . " Fifteen minutes later we know what we think—we probably already knew—but we haven't the slightest idea of how the speaker explained the position we don't like.

One way to become a better listener is to take careful notes. But that is not practical in every situation, such as when you are in conversation with others. The only sure way that works in every situation is to exercise old-fashioned self-discipline, fix your attention on what is being said, and drag your mind back the moment it starts to wander.

Good-Habit Builder

Reflect on situations in which you have had difficulty listening. Identify the kinds of distractions that are most troublesome for you. Then, whenever you are in a listening situation, be alert for those distractions. Refuse to give in to them when they arise.

Study Effective Writers

Some authors, like some speakers, gain a large and appreciative following. The reason is partly what they say, but also the way they say it. Most of us have heard from early childhood that writing is an art, and we've heard authors referred to as "gifted" and "blessed with talent." As a result, we may look at them with awe and consider what they do a wonderful but impenetrable mystery. The idea that we should analyze their work, identify their strategies, and employ them ourselves may seem almost sacrilegious.

That attitude doesn't serve us well. Writers are, after all, flesh and blood, and it takes nothing away from their achievement to realize that while the source of their inspiration may in some cases be mysterious, what they do with it is a process anyone can learn.

A single example will illustrate how much we can learn from a close reading of an effective writer. The passage is from Robert Fulghum's best-selling book, *All I Really Need to Know I Learned in Kindergarten.* The particular essay I'll quote from begins with a reference to an article the author once read about the Solomon Islanders' practice of felling trees by yelling at them. He goes on to say:

> Ah, those poor naïve innocents. Such quaintly charming habits of the jungle. Screaming at trees, indeed. How primitive. Too bad they don't have the advantages of modern technology and the scientific mind.

> Me? I yell at my wife. And yell at the telephone and the lawnmower. And yell at the TV and the newspaper and my children. I've even been known to shake my fist and yell at the sky at times.
>
> Man next door yells at his car a lot. And this summer I heard him yell at a stepladder for most of an afternoon. We modern, urban, educated folks yell at traffic and umpires and bills and banks and machines—especially machines. Machines and relatives get most of the yelling.
>
> Don't know what good it does. Machines and things just sit there. Even kicking doesn't always help. As for people, well, the Solomon Islanders may have a point. Yelling at living things does tend to kill the spirit in them. Sticks and stones may break our bones, but words will break our hearts. . . . [7]

Notice how short the sentences are. Many of them aren't even complete sentences, but fragments. They suggest informality, folksiness, and cracker-barrel philosophy. Notice too that he sets us up for his message by *saying* we know so much more than the Solomon Islanders and then demonstrating that we can learn something from them. And notice the number of typical examples of our behavior he packs into a few lines. Finally, notice how he withholds his main idea until the very end and uses a play on the words of an old saying to express it.

You can use any one of these techniques in your own writing. Of course, not all of them will be appropriate for every piece of work. (If you were writing a business report or a letter to the editor of a scholarly journal, you'd use complete sentences instead of fragments.) But some would be appropriate, and, joined with techniques that are waiting to be borrowed from other writers, they'd make your writing more effective.

Good-Habit Builder

Make a brief list of writers whose style impresses you. Include a variety of types, if possible: fiction, nonfiction essays, letters, and business or professional writing. Then examine one piece of writing, looking for effective techniques you can use in your own work.

Overcome Writer's Block

You sharpen twelve pencils, open a ream of paper, sit down in the chair, pick up a pencil, write a few words, then wait for the next thought . . . and wait . . . and wait. Writer's block can be painful; it's the real reason many people hate writing.

"If only I could have the ideas down on paper before I started writing," you may wish. Guess what? You can. That happens to be the best way to overcome writer's block—to start gathering thoughts long before the actual writing occasion, so the job of writing is not "What will I say?" but "How will I expand and organize what I've already decided to say?"

Try to anticipate writing situations as far in advance as you can. Then keep a pencil and paper handy wherever you go and be ready to capture the ideas that come to you. As you probably have already learned, they often come at unexpected times, such as while in the shower, traveling to work, or just before falling to sleep at night. Your notes needn't be neat or phrased in complete sentences. Just write enough to recall the idea when you wish.

By using this approach, you'll find that when the time comes to do the actual writing, much of what you want to say will already be on paper.

Good-Habit Builder

Decide what writing you'll do for the next week. Include personal as well as business writing. For each piece of writing, start a list of ideas to be included. Include as many ideas as you can for each. Then continue to add to the lists, from time to time, as the week progresses.

Be Economical

Somewhere in their education many people get the idea that big words are more impressive than small and that long, windy sentences and paragraphs will impress others. Both notions are false. Memorable writing is always lean and hard: consider JFK's "Ask not what your country can do for you; ask what you can do for your country" and Franklin Roosevelt's "The only thing we have to fear is fear itself."

The Gettysburg Address, one of history's great examples of economical expression, contains a total of 267 words. Of those, 217, or 81 percent, are words of one syllable. And another 32 are two-syllable words. As the proverb points out, with admirable economy, "Brevity is the soul of wit."

To gain economy in your writing (and speaking), observe the following rules. (The first two are borrowed from British author George Orwell.)

Never use a long word where a short word will do. If a long word is more appropriate for the idea, occasion, or audience, then use it. But prefer the shorter word whenever it will work as well.

Never use a foreign phrase, a scientific word, or jargon if you can think of an everyday English equivalent. Unless you are writing for specialists in your field—in which case this rule would not apply—technical language will detract from your message. If you say, "The ascendancy of the affective domain in education has compromised the position of the cognitive domain," your readers will have to make a greater effort at understanding than if you say, "The emphasis on feeling in education has weakened the place of thought." In this age of specialization, the temptation to use jargon can be strong. Resist that temptation.

Wherever possible without sacrificing effectiveness, reduce a clause to a phrase, a phrase to a word. Here are some examples of such reduction:

Inflated	Deflated
in the amount of	for
in connection with	about
on the occasion of	of
in the area of	in
I would like to request that	please
on the basis of	on
there are many cases in which	in many cases
at the present time	now
afford an opportunity to	allow
offered instruction to	taught
hold a meeting	meet
of a confidential nature	confidential

Good-Habit Builder

Select a piece of business or personal writing you did recently, or one you are now working on. Look for places where it can be improved by applying the rules explained above. Revise it accordingly.

Aim for Liveliness

When writing is dull and repetitive, it is not for lack of a "natural gift" but because the writer doesn't know, or hasn't applied, the right strategies. You can make your prose livelier by following these suggestions.

Find a fresh way to express the idea. The less predictable your expression, the easier it is to maintain your readers' interest. Here are some examples of fresh expression:

> People who are a little more hard-headed, humorous, and
> intellectually independent see the rather simple joke [of
> self-praise in advertising]. . . . If you had said to a man in
> the Stone Age, "Ugg says Ugg makes the best stone hatch-
> ets," he would have perceived a lack of detachment and
> disinterestedness about the testimonial. If you had said to
> a medieval peasant, "Robert the Bowyer proclaims, with
> three blasts of a horn, that he makes good bows," the
> peasant would have said, "Well, of course he does," and
> thought about something more important.
> —G. K. Chesterton

> It was a time when five dums and a doobie-doobie could
> make chart-busters out of incompetent hog callers with a
> three-note range.
> —Rex Reed

Substitute active voice for passive voice. Active voice
preserves the natural order of action: "Edna bought the
car." Passive voice inverts the natural order: "The car
was bought by Edna." There are times when passive
voice is preferable, such as when the focus is on what
was done rather than who did it or when you either
don't know who did it or don't care to say: "The crime
was committed last Thursday." But it's best not to let
passive voice dominate because you'll make the reader
work harder to grasp your meaning and your writing will
be less lively.

Put yourself in the background. Nothing is more boring to readers than writers who parade themselves in
their writing. The way to avoid this is to keep your use
of *I, me, mine,* and *myself* to the absolute minimum.

Vary sentence length, structure, and word order.
When all your sentences seem alike, the result is monot-

ony. Adding variety increases liveliness. If most of your sentences are short, create an occasional longer sentence by combining two or three. If all your sentences begin the same way, alter the word order as the following examples illustrate:

Original	Revision
I really believed, for one brief moment, that he was serious.	For one brief moment, I really believed that he was serious.
Marie was dejected and sat in a corner by herself all evening.	Dejected, Marie sat in a corner by herself all evening.
The best time to begin saving money is now.	Now is the best time to begin saving money.
It is foolish and dangerous to try to lose that much weight in just a few weeks.	To try to lose that much weight in just a few weeks is foolish and dangerous.
We plan to travel to Europe this summer if we can afford it.	If we can afford it, we plan to travel to Europe this summer.

Good-Habit Builder

Select a piece of writing you did recently or are working on now. Improve its liveliness by finding a fresh expression, substituting active for passive voice, putting yourself in the background, and/or varying your sentences.

8

Habits
for Moral Character

The modern notion about progress suggests that knowledge is ever deepening, yesterday's understanding is passé, and anything believed a hundred years ago is archaic and without merit. That notion is rooted in intellectual pride and frequently leads us into error. A noteworthy example of such error can be found in much current writing about morality. The subject is popular: Newspapers and magazines headline the moral lapses of elected officials, the business community, and assorted celebrities. Editorials and letters to the editor regularly urge that moral values be added to school curriculums. However, most people avoid getting very specific about what should be taught and how. They seem to assume that memorizing names and dates and being able to recite the Ten Commandments will by some magic produce moral people. And therein lies the error.

Although factual knowledge is valuable, there is little or no correlation between knowing better and living better lives. People can know right from wrong and yet rob, and rape, and even murder. And surely corrupt politicians, insider traders on Wall Street, and the savings and loan officials who misused that industry and threw the country further into debt were not ignorant of the nature and consequences of their actions. They just didn't care.

It is not sufficient to honor virtue in the abstract; we must practice it in everyday life. The key to producing moral people, as the ancients knew and we in our pride have forgotten, is motivating them to want to behave morally and helping them form the habits of thought and action associated with right conduct.

Develop Your Conscience

Everyday experience demonstrates that conscience is not equally sensitive in everyone. Some people are acutely aware when they do wrong. They ask forgiveness of the one they have offended, promise not to repeat the offense, and make good on their promise. The more we get to know them, and the more they share their confidences with us, the more impressed we are at the depth of their moral sensitivity.

Then there are people who are morally sensitive in some areas but not in others. They recognize that it is wrong to steal, but they are blind to the wrongness of lying. Or they feel guilty about taking the Lord's name in vain but not about treating their families cruelly.

Still others seem to lack a conscience altogether. They show no sign of remorse and seem unaware and unconcerned about the effects of their actions on others. They do as they wish, when they wish, and feel no compunction for so doing. The language of morality—"obligations," "ideals," "consequences of actions"—is absent from their conversation and from their lexicon. Judging from reports of antisocial behavior, the number of people in this group seems to be increasing.

Because conscience can differ so widely in its level of development, it is foolish to trust conscience implicitly and follow it without question. Chances are it has been corrupted by the reigning philosophy of self and needs to be developed, sharpened, and sensitized before it can provide the moral guidance we need.

One way to develop your conscience is to ponder the Ten Commandments, probing their relevance to our age. What does it mean to have other gods than God? What things are people tempted to put before God and worship instead of Him? . . . How does God want us to observe the Sabbath? By simply not working? By engaging in family activities? By attending church or spending extra time in prayer? . . . What words or actions constitute honoring our parents? What ones constitute dishonoring them? . . . What thoughts, words, and deeds violate the letter or the spirit of the commandment to refrain from adultery? . . . What specific activities constitute stealing? (Is stealing limited to material things?) . . . In what ways are people tempted to bear false witness against their neighbors? . . . Where is the line between admiring other people's goods or spouses and coveting them?

Another way to develop your conscience is to reflect on the beatitudes and their application to modern life.

> Blessed are the poor in spirit. . . . Blessed are those who mourn. . . . Blessed are the gentle. . . . Blessed are those who hunger and thirst for righteousness. . . . Blessed are the merciful. . . . Blessed are the poor in heart. . . . Blessed are the peacemakers. . . . Blessed are those who have been persecuted for the sake of righteousness. . . . Blessed are you when men . . . persecute you . . . on account of me.
>
> —Matthew 5:3–11

> Woe to you who are rich. . . . Woe to you who are well-fed now. . . . Woe to you when all men speak well of you. . . . Love your enemies, do good to those who hate you, bless those who curse you, pray for those who mistreat you. Whoever hits you on the cheek, offer him the other also. . . . Give to everyone who asks of you. . . . And just as you want people to treat you, treat them in the same

way. . . . Love your enemies, and do good, and lend, expecting nothing in return. . . . Be merciful, just as your
Father is merciful. And do not judge . . . do not condemn
. . . pardon [others]. . . . Give, and it will be given to you.
. . . First take the log out of your own eye, and then you
will see clearly to take out the speck that is in your
brother's eye.

—Luke 6:24–42

Good-Habit Builder

Keep the Ten Commandments and the beatitudes on
your mind as you go through your daily activities, including your reading and TV viewing. Ask yourself
where people should be ashamed of their behavior and
feel remorse (whether they react this way or not).

Identify Your Moral Offenses

Popular psychology proclaims that it is harmful to
think about our past offenses. Such thoughts, it is believed, make us feel bad about ourselves and lose our
self-esteem. This view is a dangerous half-truth. Of
course, it's possible to be morbidly preoccupied with
past offenses, to carry them as a burden that blocks
moral growth and leads to depression and despair. But
fear of that extreme reaction is vastly overemphasized
today. Given our culture's advocacy of instant gratification and self-justification, it is more reasonable to fear
chronic insensitivity to our faults than oversensitivity.

Nothing makes us feel worse about ourselves—at a
deep spiritual level, if not consciously—than doing
wrong. The first step in removing that feeling is to acknowledge what we have done. Refusing to do so usually
leads to lying to ourselves ("It wasn't my fault," or "She
deserved it"), and there's nothing healthy or positive
about that.

The Judeo-Christian perspective on the matter is nicely summed up in a Russian proverb: "Make peace with [other people] and quarrel with your faults." To put this sensible prescription into practice, develop the habit of reviewing your moral offenses at least once a week. Identify and acknowledge precisely what wrongs you did. Don't try to escape feeling ashamed and remorseful; they are appropriate sentiments. Face them humbly.

Your aim is not to hate yourself for what you did, but to hate what you did and motivate yourself to avoid doing it again. Get beyond "What could I have done? I had no alternative." Realize that you probably had a number of alternatives but either didn't think of them or deliberately ignored them.

Good-Habit Builder

Identify the offenses you have committed in the past week. Apply your creativity and think of the various alternatives that were open to you at the time, things you could have said or done to avoid doing wrong.

Know Where You Are Vulnerable

Before we commit an immoral act, we first experience temptation. At times it will occur suddenly—"Take that pen; no one will know"—and then quickly subside. At others it will be more persistent, taunting, nagging, cajoling us for hours or longer. The best preparation for either assault is to know which moral offenses we are most susceptible to and in what circumstances we are most vulnerable to them.

The seven deadly sins are pride, coveteousness, lust, anger, gluttony, envy, and sloth. Each represents a broad category of offenses. Few people are severely tempted by all of them. One person may experience

powerful temptations to anger, only occasional temptations to lust or sloth, and no temptation to the others.

Many people are very clear about their neighbors'
temptations but uncertain of their own. This is because
they have developed the habit of maximizing their neighbors' faults and minimizing (if not outright excusing) their
own. As a result, they are more likely than others to be
caught off guard by temptation and succumb to it.

The best way to resist temptation is to anticipate it by
answering the following questions: What moral offenses
have you been tempted to in the past? In what circumstances have those temptations occurred? When you
were alone? With certain individuals? At home? In
school? In the office? At particular times of the day? Did
certain emotional states—anger, for example, or elation,
depression or self-pity—trigger temptations? Does ex-
haustion increase your vulnerability? Does alcohol?

Because the act of writing has a way of stimulating
thought, answering these questions on paper may provide insights not usually produced by thinking alone. It's
a good idea to put your answers where no one is likely to
find them. If you feel you need a more visible reminder,
create a code word such as WOT for "work on temper,"
write it on a piece of paper, and post it where you will
see it several times a day.

Next, decide how to avoid the temptation, or at least
overcome it when it arises. Consider avoiding offending
places and people. If there is no practical way to do that,
think of how you can best resist the temptation: by
changing the discussion, perhaps, or saying a silent
prayer, or forming a mental picture of Jesus, a parent,
your spouse, or a special friend.

Good-Habit Builder

Make a list of your strongest temptations and decide
how you can best overcome each.

Overcome Procrastination

Procrastination is the polar opposite of action. It thrives on excuses, such as "The timing isn't quite right yet" and "I'm too busy just now, but soon . . . " Many people try to overcome procrastination by strengthening their good intentions. Unfortunately, as the proverb wisely notes, "The road to hell is paved with good intentions." In fact, intentions can actually *cause* us to procrastinate. Once we resolve to do something good, like writing someone a letter of thanks or making a generous donation to the poor, we usually feel a sense of completeness, of satisfaction. And the more noble the intention, the stronger this feeling can be.

Somehow, "I've decided to" acquires the force of "I have." Although at one level we know they aren't the same, at another level we don't. Anticipation of accomplishment becomes confused with actual accomplishment, and our motivation to accomplish is diminished.

The first step in overcoming procrastination is to admit that we are better defined by our actions than our intentions. Jesus didn't say, By their intentions you shall know them, but "By their fruits [actions] you shall know them." Wanting to do, yearning to do, hoping and planning and promising to do are nothing but a preface to doing, a wispy dream without substance.

Remembering this fact will prepare you for the next, decisive step: taking action. Once you have formed an intention, do something about it immediately. If the matter is important, it is worth making time for. Take pen in hand and write that letter of thanks or send that donation. If your intended letter is too long to write at this time, write a brief note and write the longer version later. How much time does it take to say, "I never told you, but I always admired you and your example continues to inspire me," and to address an envelope?

Even if your intention involves significant effort over a long period of time, there is no reason not to make a small beginning immediately and to build on it at the earliest opportunity. Do that, and you will conquer procrastination.

Good-Habit Builder

For the next few days, whenever you find yourself saying "I'm going to do that . . . " add "right now" and then take action. If action is truly impossible in some cases, don't worry; it will be enough to take immediate action in the other cases. Keep a tally of your successes.

Note Obligations, Ideals, Consequences

We know why we are commanded to love our neighbor: because regardless of his or her race, social status, ethnic background, behavior, or station in life, our neighbor is created in the image and likeness of God, a person and not a thing. Yet it is not always easy to tell what exactly is required of us in the myriad situations that arise in everyday living. "What should I do in this situation?" we wonder. "Exactly what action will constitute loving the people involved?" The best way to answer these questions is to examine the relevant obligations and ideals and consider the consequences of the actions open to us.

Obligations arise from formal agreements, such as contracts to perform a service or provide a product. They are also created by significant relationships, such as that of husband and wife, child and parent, brother and sister, employer and employee. There are also professional obligations and those of citizenship and friendship.

Ideals are kinds of behavioral excellence. The most

common and important ones include justice, fairness, tolerance, compassion, loyalty, forgiveness, harmony, and mutual understanding.

Consequences are the effects produced by an action. They include the physical, emotional, and spiritual and may affect the person taking the action, other people, or both. Often consequences are not obvious but subtle, not immediate but delayed. In some situations they can't be predicted with certainty, so we must decide on the basis of probability: What seems most likely to happen, given the circumstances.

Many moral issues are complex, involving two or more *conflicting* obligations or ideals. For example, our obligation to an employer may demand that we keep his illegal business practices confidential, whereas the ideal of honesty compels us to report those practices to law officials. In this case, we must decide which is the higher obligation.

Similarly, the consequences of an action may be not all good or bad, but mixed. Tightening pollution standards will improve air quality and reduce acid rain, but create prohibitive cost increases for factories and eliminate jobs. On the other hand, not tightening pollution standards will have favorable consequences for factory owners and workers, yet will worsen air quality and perpetuate the problem of acid rain. Our dilemma is that neither choice of action is completely acceptable. In such cases, we must decide which action will produce the greater good or, at very least, the lesser harm.

Good-Habit Builder

Consider an action you or someone else already took, or one you are contemplating, that you are not sure is moral. Examine the obligations, ideals, and consequences and decide whether the action is moral.

Give the Benefit of the Doubt

A friend of mine, an accomplished professional, shared this story with me. He and his wife had met and married late in life, after both had lost their spouses. His wife's sister occasionally telephoned her and, if he answered the telephone, she would say, "Is Carol there?" Every time this occurred, his resentment grew, and finally he said to his wife, "What is the matter with that woman? We've stayed at her house and she's stayed at ours. She knows me. Can't she have the decency to address me by name? Is it so hard to say, 'Hello, Frank, this is Edith; may I please speak to Carol'?"

For the next couple of weeks, whenever the sister's name came up, Frank renewed his tirade. And when she called and repeated the offense, his anger escalated. "She dislikes me, and that's her way of showing it. There's no other explanation. She's rude and contemptible, and someday I'm going to tell her what I think of her behavior."

He never did tell her because, the next time they met, she confided in him that she felt in awe of him. "Your achievements are so impressive," she explained, "that I feel nervous in your presence. I know it's silly of me, but I've actually felt tongue-tied when I've spoken to you." At that moment, he told me later, he felt very small indeed.

Giving the benefit of the doubt is difficult when our pride is shaken and our ego ruffled. Nevertheless, in any case where we cannot be certain why a person behaved in a certain way, and that means the vast majority of cases, we should be generous in our assessment and think the best. Reacting this way is a practical way to observe Jesus' admonition, "Do not judge lest you be judged."

An even better way is to use our imagination and think of a plausible explanation for the behavior. Here are just a few of the many possibilities Frank could have considered: "Edith may not have been thinking." "Perhaps she was preoccupied with a personal problem at work or some difficulty in her marriage." "It could be she is suffering from a serious ailment that no one else knows about." "Maybe she was worrying over trouble besetting her husband or her children." (In any of these circumstances, she could easily have been completely unaware of committing an offense.)

But what if no such explanation is plausible; what if an action is so grievous and so obviously intentional that you can find no honest way to excuse it? In that case, you can consider the possibility that the person has since realized the import of the action, has felt ashamed, and may now be saying, "What a fool I am to behave so meanly and threaten a relationship I value."

Good-Habit Builder

Recall a recent offense someone committed against you. Reconsider your reaction to it, doing your best to give the offender the benefit of the doubt.

Speak Well of Others

"Goodbye. Thanks for a nice time. We'll see you soon," Jack says, as he closes his car door and drives away. Then, before he and Alice are finished waving out the window, he's begun the attack. "I can't believe she got that promotion. She doesn't have the qualifications for it. She must have buttered up the boss."

"They always seem to have things go their way," Alice adds. "And it certainly isn't because they're more industrious than others. Did you notice how messy their house is? The kitchen is a disaster area."

"Yeah, and they don't do such a good job of parenting either. Did you notice how their son . . . ?"

On and on it goes. When they arrive home twenty minutes later they're still busily tearing their hosts apart. And tomorrow they'll repeat their remarks to co-workers and neighbors. Of course, they don't think of what they do as gossiping, and they'd be outraged if anyone described it that way. Like so many other people, they fail to realize that dwelling on others' real or imagined faults and sharing negative stories with others are violations of friendship. They never consider that their tongues have the potential to ruin people's reputations and injure relationships.

The best reason for overcoming the gossiping habit and speaking well of others is that doing so is a sign of character. As Ann Landers is fond of saying, "Superior people talk about ideas. Mediocre people talk about things. Small people talk about other people."

But there are other good reasons, as well. Gossiping is not only a tremendous waste of time, it also withers our optimism and sours our view of life. Moreover, since intelligent people know that if we gossip to them about others, we will gossip to others about them, it can make them lose respect for us and ultimately threaten our relationship with them.

To break this hateful habit, make a conscious effort to speak well of others. Look for positive characteristics in others—everyone has some—and talk about them. If the people you are talking to focus on the negative, turn the conversation back to the positive. And any time you can't think of anything positive to say about the person under discussion, remain silent or change the subject.

Good-Habit Builder

Make a special effort today to monitor your conversation. Be alert for the temptation to gossip and if it occurs, make yourself speak well of others.

Be a "Gentleperson"

A "gentleperson" is someone who never knowingly causes another pain. Such a person is not very fashionable today. The modern counsel is "Stand up for your rights," "Don't let people take advantage of you," "Look out for number one." Few modern people fear being overly aggressive and hurting other people's feelings. Rather, they fear being wimps.

Being a gentleperson doesn't mean being spineless or refusing to speak out on matters of principle. It means applying the Golden Rule in your relationships with others: avoiding confrontations and meeting rudeness with civility, impatience with patience, meanness with kindness.

There is no better expression of the gentleperson's credo than the well-known prayer of Francis of Assisi:

> Lord, make me an instrument of your peace.
>   Where there is hatred, let me sow love;
>   Where there is injury, pardon;
>   Where there is doubt, faith;
>   Where there is despair, hope;
>   Where there is darkness, light;
>   Where there is sadness, joy.
> O Divine Master, grant that I may not so much seek
>   to be consoled as to console,
>   to be understood as to understand,
>   to be loved as to love.
> For it is in giving that we receive,
>   it is in pardoning that we are pardoned,
>   and it is in dying that we are born to eternal life.

Good-Habit Builder

Reflect on the prayer of St. Francis and think of everyday situations in which you can sow love, pardon, faith, hope, light, and joy; and in which you can console, understand, and love.

9

Habits
for Craftsmanship

In the past few years concern over excellence has been growing. Consumers continue to complain about inferior goods and services. In a desperate search for ways to improve quality control, business leaders have adopted strategies for worker involvement in decision making, added profit-sharing plans, and fine-tuned their hiring practices. The publishing industry has responded to the problem with detailed descriptions of successful people and companies. The seminar industry offers inspiration and motivation.

These laudable efforts have generally been unsuccessful. Not surprisingly. Popular culture promotes mediocrity. The heroes held up for emulation are entertainers, and not always the most technically accomplished ones. The emphasis is not on becoming excellent in a field but on making a lot of money, not on earning respect for one's work but on achieving celebrity the easiest way possible. In the media, including the publishing industry, a gimmick or hook is more sought after than genuine artistry. In this age of advertising, with its standard approach of "selling the sizzle, not the steak," is it any wonder that appearance has become more important than reality?

Excellence is found only where there is a sense of craftsmanship—that is, where the people involved take pride in their work and invest whatever effort is necessary to make it the best it can be. Craftsmanship is refusing to cut corners or hide second-rate work in glitter and bombast. It is, in a word, caring about what we do.

Reflect on the Importance of Your Work

"Enthusiasm is the electricity of life," observes author and film director Gordon Parks. "How do you get it? You act enthusiastic until you make it a habit. Enthusiasm is natural; it is being alive, taking the initiative, seeing the importance of what you do, giving it dignity, and making what you do important to yourself and others."

While London's famous St. Paul's Cathedral was being built, a visitor asked two workmen what they were doing. One replied, "Cutting stone"; the other, "Helping to build a cathedral." It is not known which of the two did finer work, but this much is certain: The second worker was more likely to have the sense of the importance of his work, and the enthusiasm, that Parks extolled.

We often tend to see the worth only of other people's work, not our own. We think of our own work in terms of its endless routines, its annoying complications, its drudgery. That perspective is one reason that so many people hate their work, seek every excuse to absent themselves from the workplace, and content themselves with mediocre performance.

Which person is more likely to achieve excellence, the fast-food worker who thinks, "I take food orders" or the one who thinks, "I serve people their meals"? The dentist who thinks, "I put fillings in people's teeth" or the one who thinks, "I make teeth healthy, relieve pain, and make people smile"? The salesperson who thinks, "I sell this product or service," or the one who thinks, "I help people make purchases that will bring them satisfaction"?

"The secret of life," England's King George V observed, "is not to do what one likes, but to try to like what one has to do." The key to liking what you do is to focus on its importance, the contribution it makes, great or small, to some larger effort, to other people, to the world.

Good-Habit Builder

Consider the tasks you perform, not just in your formal occupation but also in your other roles, as spouse, parent, neighbor, community volunteer. Select one and reflect on its importance. If it is only a small part of some larger job, reflect on the importance of that job. Decide how you can maintain this positive perspective while you are performing this task.

Extend Your Concentration

A few years ago, I did an informal study of the shifts in attention forced on viewers during a half hour of television. The show was a soap opera, and I counted as a shift the movement from one couple's dilemma to another's, from a present scene to a past one (flashback) or to a fantasy, as well as the movement to a commercial break and then from one commercial to another. (Today the standard is four commercials per minute.) I also counted the movement to "newsbreaks," which used to be reserved for news items too important to delay but now are used as commercials for the next regular newscast, saying in effect, Tune in to our news show tonight—we'll have some news for you.

In all I tallied 39 attention shifts in thirty minutes. In other words, viewers' attention was being forced to change at a rate of 78 times per hour! A quick survey of other programming will confirm that the rate is little different there. No wonder students grow impatient when the teacher focuses on a point for more than a minute or two. No wonder reading is on the decline and listening is fast becoming a lost art. No wonder quality control is a problem in business. And no wonder professional services often fail to meet reasonable expectations.

Craftsmanship demands concentration. And the more complicated or technical your work, the greater that concentration must be. If you have been exposed to television for a number of years, your concentration has undoubtedly diminished without your realizing it. Here are some approaches you can take to restore and extend it.

Watch less television and, when you do watch, choose shows with few commercial interruptions or none at all.

Spend some time reading every day. Visit the library and get a work of fiction or, if you prefer, nonfiction. Consider selecting a book about your field of work or parenting or a subject you have always wanted to learn more about but never found time to explore.

Take up a hobby, particularly one that demands close attention, such as painting or pottery or woodworking.

Be prepared to find yourself losing patience with what you are doing. It is a natural enough result of living years with a shortened attention span. Whenever you feel the urge to zap aimlessly around the television channels or to shift your attention from viewing, reading, or working, force yourself to extend your concentration.

Good-Habit Builder

Don't let yourself say, "Good ideas—I'm going to follow them as soon as I have time." Make time. Put one or all of these suggestions to work for you today.

Learn from Others

My friend's son Edgar had just graduated from college with a major in restaurant management and was about to enter the field as assistant manager of a restaurant. In addition to technical training, he possessed two other prerequisites for success in the field: a friendly manner and the desire to please. Yet Edgar had one habit that threatened his chances of success: Whenever anyone, such as his supervisor on a part-time job, would try to explain how to do something, Edgar would claim to know how to do it already, whether he knew or not, in an effort to impress the person.

Edgar's father had a long talk with him before he began his new job, pointing out the wisdom of accepting instruction, mastering the tasks assigned to him, and performing them to the best of his ability. "When others offer to explain something to you or show you how to do it, listen carefully. Demonstrating that you can learn from others is the most basic way to impress your employer. Once you have made that impression, you can go on to demonstrate your other talents, such as creativity."

Six months later, I asked the father how Edgar was doing. He replied that Edgar had lost his job, mainly, it seemed, because he had pretended he knew how to do something and, as a result, had made a costly error.

It may be possible to achieve craftsmanship solely through one's own experience, making all one's own mistakes, never profiting from what others have learned, but it certainly isn't the easiest or most practical way. Life is too short; there simply isn't enough time. It is much more sensible to adopt the approach taken by the great artists and artisans of medieval Europe, the approach still practiced in many Asian countries, including Japan: the apprentice approach. This needn't mean attaching oneself to a single master craftsman, it may simply mean continuing to be a student of the field (regardless of how much schooling you have had) and humbling yourself to learn from anyone who has achieved mastery.

The years spent mastering any field, from cooking to counseling, plumbing to brain surgery, are filled with blunders as well as successful efforts. By consulting the men and women who have achieved mastery, you can learn not only what strategies are most efficient and productive but also what mistakes to avoid. Thus you can save yourself time and frustration.

Most achievers, even people of distinction, are willing to share their insights with others. All it takes to gain these priceless gifts is the humility to admit you don't know everything and a willingness to learn from others.

Good-Habit Builder

Determine in what areas you could stand to learn from others' experience: for example, at work, in your marriage, in parenting. Decide what questions you would like to find answers to and where you can find those answers. If someone you know has relevant expertise, call that person and make an appointment to talk with him or her. If you don't know anyone, ask your reference librarian how to find helpful books and articles. Take this first step today.

Aim for Excellence in Small Things

Recently a friend of mine bought a suit. Alterations, he was promised, would be completed by Thursday noon. After work on Thursday, he drove to the store. The salesman explained that the tailor had been unusually busy and the suit wouldn't be ready until Friday. On Friday, another trip and another disappointment. The salesman gave his solemn oath the suit would be ready on Saturday.

His word proved good. On Saturday the suit was ready, but the alterations had been completely botched.

Yesterday in the grocery store the cash register

showed a total of $14.26. I gave the clerk a twenty-dollar bill and a penny. She entered $20.01 in the machine, read the correct change indicated there ($5.75), and proceeded to hand me a five-dollar bill, two quarters, one nickel, and two pennies.

One reason shoddy performance is so common today is that many people have their eyes too much on the future. They see their present jobs as temporary, mere stepping-stones to their ultimate goals. "It doesn't really matter how I perform here," they reason. "When I get the job I really want, I'll love what I do, so naturally I'll excel."

That's just wishful thinking. Because habits are not easily broken, people who perform poorly on their present jobs are likely to do so on future jobs, no matter how enjoyable they find them. More importantly, people with poor work records are not likely to get the jobs they seek, particularly if those jobs involve heavier responsibility or more complex work. "Show me a man who cannot bother to do little things," writes Jacob M. Braude, "and I'll show you a man who can't be trusted to do big things."

Imagine how foolish it would be for a man to look so single-mindedly for $100 bills that, when he found $1, $5, $10, or $20 bills, he threw them away. People are behaving just as foolishly when they squander thousands of small opportunities to practice excellence while they wait for the one monumental chance to prove themselves on a heroic scale.

The fact is the big chance may never come. Life comes to us on its own terms, not ours, and we have no way of knowing what lies ahead. But of this much we can be certain: The only possibilities for excellence many of us will encounter will be the little ones. If we are wise, we will refuse to waste precious time daydreaming of things that may never be while ignoring those that are. We will seize all those little opportunities. No matter how small

the job, or whether someone else will see the finished
work or not, we will do it so well that we'd be willing to
have it stand as the measure of ourselves.

If we find the future holds a greater challenge, we will
be better prepared for it for having done our best on
innumerable smaller, more manageable tasks. And if no
greater challenge comes, our effort will still not have
been wasted. Excellence will have been a reality for us,
not just an idle dream.

Good-Habit Builder

Select a small task you do quite frequently and hur-
riedly, with little thought for the quality of your performance. Consider tasks at work and those at home. For
the latter consider, among other activities, writing letters to friends and relatives, washing the car, shining
shoes, ironing, making your bed, cooking, serving food,
dressing, conversing, and folding clothes.

Decide how you can improve the way you perform
the task. In letter writing, you might polish your pen-
manship or include more descriptive details. As you do
the task, concentrate on that improvement. The idea is
to focus on achieving excellence while you are working.
When you have finished, appraise your performance. If
appropriate, make a mental note on how to do even better next time. Gradually extend your focus on excellence
to all your other activities.

At the outset you will probably find that aiming for
excellence results in spending more time on each activity. Don't be concerned about that. You can learn to
combine excellence and efficiency.

Allow Sufficient Lead Time

"My term paper is due by Friday and I haven't even
begun it yet." Did you ever find yourself saying that

when you were in school? For many people those words are merely a rehearsal for adult experience. Now they say, "The proposal is due tomorrow. I'll have to rush to get it done"; "I'm supposed to make a presentation at this afternoon's meeting, and I haven't even thought what I'll say"; "There's no way I'm going to get my annual report done on time."

It makes sense to avoid such situations whenever possible, for haste is the enemy of excellence.

The best way to avoid hasty efforts is to start every project early, as soon as it is assigned or you decide to do it. Devise a strategy immediately, being sure to specify what investigation or research will be necessary and how you will conduct it. Record your preliminary ideas. If possible, rough out how the final product will look. As long as you remain flexible, there's little danger that early planning will compromise your creativity later.

Next, make a place for the project in your schedule. If you are a busy person, you're not likely to find a free block of three or four hours, so don't bother looking. Instead, look for a number of smaller blocks. The time you spend waiting to do other things, such as waiting for appointments, is ideal. Just be sure to carry the necessary project materials with you, so you'll be ready to work on it in spare moments.

Whenever possible, set a personal deadline for the project. Make it at least a week or two earlier than the actual completion date, so you'll have ample time to refine your work and to deal with the complications and delays that may arise.

Good-Habit Builder

Select an assignment you've recently been given, or have chosen, but haven't yet begun. Begin working on it today. Determine what you'll have to do to complete the assignment, exactly where you'll fit it into your schedule, and what your own personal deadline will be. Keep this plan in a prominent place, so that you'll remember to follow it.

Find More to Do

Many people have a piecework mentality—they work very well when they are given something to do, but when that project is finished they sit and wait for another to be assigned. In time this habit can lead to spreading the work—working more slowly than necessary because they don't want to be sitting with nothing to do. Their problem is that they have never learned to take the initiative and find things to do, and it prevents them from achieving excellence.

The idea of excellence extends beyond the quality of individual pieces of our work. It covers, too, our whole attitude toward what we do. The real craftsperson not only produces fine work but achieves as much quantity as possible consistent with quality.

Whenever you have extra time on your hands, put it to good use. Look for a task that is not being done and do it. If you can't find such a task, invest the time in learning some new aspect of the field or studying new approaches. Bring books to work that help you learn; read them, when time permits, so that you can broaden your skills and expand the contribution you make.

This notion, to be sure, runs counter to the prevailing wisdom, which says, "Do what they pay you to do, nothing more, and don't rush in doing it." Some employers have grown to tolerate, even expect, such an approach to work. There may even be some who will not look kindly on the approach recommended here.

Nevertheless, most employers will find this attitude on your part laudable and will reward you for it. More important, you will feel a greater sense of pride and accomplishment. As a bonus, your day will go faster; no torture is quite so exquisite as that of staring at the clock, waiting for quitting time.

Good-Habit Builder

Think of situations at work when you can do something extra or can use your time more productively and expand your expertise. Decide what you will do with that time.

Lose Yourself in Your Work

Thinking skills researcher George Humphrey tells the story of the man who told his nephew that if he did better in school he would take him to the zoo to see the lions fed. The boy began working feverishly, and his marks improved dramatically; in fact, he was so conscientious he grew ill. His parents naturally became worried and inquired why he had been working so hard. It seemed the boy had misunderstood his uncle. He had thought that, unless he improved, he would be fed to the lions.

Terror can provide powerful motivation to excellence. Fortunately, there are other motivations, such as becoming so absorbed in what you are doing that you lose yourself in your work.

That expression, "lose yourself," is most appropriate. After all, focus on self, and extensions of self, are the greatest obstacles to concentration on the job. In the mid 1950s, as a young industrial engineer and the father of three small children, I found myself spending considerable time, on the job as well as off, in a reverie that went something like this:

"I'm making $4500 now. If I get the raise I'm expecting next month I'll be making $5000. That extra $10 a week will help us afford . . .

"In two years, if I get a promotion to Supervising Engineer, I'll get an automatic $1500 raise and then we'll be able to replace the car and maybe even make a down-payment on a house. Then . . . "

When I realized what I was doing, I quickly decided that my reverie, if carelessly indulged, could actually prevent me from realizing my hopes. "Forget the daydreaming," I told myself. "Just give each assignment your full attention, and you'll increase your chances of achieving your goal." The lesson is even more valuable today, when mass media fill our heads with "lifestyles of the rich and famous" fantasies and condition us to scorn self-control.

Far from adding drudgery to your life, losing yourself in your work will make your work more enjoyable. Time spent on the job will pass more quickly. You'll accomplish more, the quality of your work will improve, and you'll derive a greater sense of satisfaction from your efforts. In time, your supervisor will recognize and acknowledge the improvement and see you as a more valuable employee, and this new perspective will increase your chances of a salary increase and a promotion.

The key to losing yourself in your work is to hang your hopes, daydreams, and fantasies on the coatrack as you enter work and pick them up again as you leave. Better yet, hang them in the closet at home and save them for special occasions. They won't lose their importance by being thus confined.

Old habits die hard, so expect to find yourself slipping back into your old daydreams. Whenever that happens, force your attention back to your work. After doing this a dozen or so times, you'll begin to notice that your concentration is increasing. If you persist, maintaining your attention will require only modest occasional effort.

Good-Habit Builder

Begin today to improve your concentration on the job. Monitor your attention, and whenever you find your mind wandering, force it back to the task at hand. Continue this effort until you find yourself becoming so absorbed in your work that others have to remind you that it's lunchtime or quitting time.

Conquer Discouragement

After laboring for five years over the first volume of *The French Revolution,* Thomas Carlyle sent the only copy to his friend John Stuart Mill, whose housemaid accidentally used it to start a fire. When Carlyle learned the manuscript was lost, he was deeply troubled. However, rather than giving in to despair, he began all over and produced a masterpiece.

Viktor Frankl, Viennese psychiatrist and inmate of the concentration camps that were to rob him of everyone in his family except his sisters, carried with him a manuscript containing his life's professional work. When he asked the guards if he could keep it, they laughed at him and forced him to discard it. Refusing to be daunted by the experience, he used the concentration camp experience as an opportunity to probe the human mind and heart.

The psychological theories of Freud and Adler, Frankl found, were mistaken. Long after the inmates' suffering had quelled their sex drive and drive for power, something more fundamental remained strong. Frankl called it our search for meaning, the drive to make sense out of our lives.

Few people face the extreme frustration, disappointment, and disillusionment that confronted Carlyle and Frankl. Yet discouragement is an inescapable part of every life. We have no control over when it will visit us or the intensity of the pain it will bring, though we can be reasonably sure that the more serious our commitment to excellence, the higher we reach, the more we are apt to suffer.

The key to conquering discouragement is to anticipate it and develop a strategy for dealing with it. Know the various forms it takes: self-pity, a feeling of hopelessness, and the temptation to give up.

When it whispers, "Poor you, others have good luck; you have only bad," make yourself recall other people's ill fortune. Press yourself to feel sorrow for them so that you will have no room for self-pity. When it mocks, "See how your efforts come to nothing," remind yourself that no honest effort is ever wasted and that trying your best is noble. And when it tells you there is no point in continuing in what you know to be a good cause, that it will be far easier to spare yourself anxiety, remind yourself that though success may elude you if you continue, you will forfeit all chance to it if you give up.

Good-Habit Builder

Identify the situations in your life that you find most discouraging. Focus on situations that tend to recur. Take the time now to plan how you can most effectively deal with each one. Write down as exactly as you can the feelings and thoughts you experience on those occasions; then construct the words that will help you conquer discouragement. Borrow the words given above, if they are appropriate.

Profit from Your Failures

My friend's thirteen-year-old son was embarking on a physical fitness program that included daily exercise in jumping rope. He bought a rope and attempted to use it, but quickly became frustrated. He couldn't jump a single time without getting hopelessly tangled in the rope. The more he tried, the more hopeless the task seemed, so he admitted defeat. "I just can't do it!" he exclaimed, and hid the jump rope in the closet.

When the boy's father learned what had happened, he explained to the boy that the ability to jump rope is not something a person is born with; it's a skill developed through long practice. "In the beginning," he said, "everyone feels as clumsy as you did. Grace has to be earned."

Encouraged by his father's words, the boy began investing fifteen minutes a day in practicing. A few weeks later, he proudly showed everyone that he could jump a hundred times without stopping.

Many adults share that boy's view of failure. They regard ability as inborn rather than acquired. "I failed at this, so obviously I lack the necessary talent to ever succeed." They are wrong; great achievers often experience many failures before succeeding.

Agatha Christie's first novel was rejected a number of times before a publisher accepted it. Louis L'Amour, famous author of western novels, received more than two hundred rejection slips before he got his first acceptance. And Dr. Seuss had his first manuscript rejected by so many publishers that he almost burned it in frustration.

Winston Churchill was the poorest student in his prep school class. He was weak in every subject, including English. Thomas Edison was told to quit school because he was stupid. He lost his first job after he set a train on fire, and his first attempt at invention was a failure. Henry Ford failed at two businesses before he established the Ford Motor Company. Abraham Lincoln failed so miserably in business it took him fifteen years to pay off his debts. When he first ran for office, he finished eighth in a field of thirteen. Then he lost two bids for the House and two for the Senate.

Albert Einstein's record of failure is even more dramatic. An unimpressive student, Einstein was told flatly by his teacher, "You will never amount to anything." At age fifteen he was asked to leave school. He proceeded to fail his first entrance exam for college and was required to spend an additional year in high school before he could be admitted. In college, he did such mediocre work that he was rejected as a postgraduate assistant and denied a recommendation for employment. Eventually he got a job as a tutor at a boarding school but was soon fired. When he submitted a thesis for a doctoral degree, it was rejected. Four years later, he submitted a new dissertation, this one on his theory of relativity. It too was rejected.

What is the secret of great achievers' ultimate success? There are, in fact, two secrets. First is the realization that failure and defeat are not synonymous. George Bernard Shaw said, "When I was a young man I observed that nine out of ten things I did were failures. I didn't want to be a failure, so I did ten times more work."

The second secret is to make the failure work for you—that is, examine it closely and determine what went wrong. Here is an approach you can use to profit from your failures.

Review all the details surrounding the effort, including the original situation that prompted you to act and the sequence of events that culminated in your failure.

Consider all possible explanations of why the failure occurred. Be sure you identify possible flaws in your plan of action and its implementation, unforeseen circumstances that may have arisen, and the lack of support or outright opposition of other people. Your goal here is to gain new insight into the failure, so if you have already made up your mind what caused it, you will have to set aside that judgment and reexamine the matter. (Avoid the error of assuming that your earlier judgment was necessarily correct.)

Decide how your failure is best explained and what action on your part would have increased your chances of success. If the matter is still open, decide what your next initiative will be.

Good-Habit Builder

Think of a recent undertaking in which you experienced failure. Review the details. Then determine what went wrong, what you should have done differently, and, if appropriate, how you will try again.

Follow Good Advice from Any Source

"My Way" is a wonderful song, stirring and inspiring, especially when sung by Frank Sinatra in his prime. But the most realistic line in the song is the last one, "The record shows I took the blows and did it my way." For anyone who takes the idea in the song as a guide for living, there will certainly be blows aplenty. Stubbornness exacts a heavy penalty. Fantasy aside, we ought to be less concerned about "my way" and more about the best and most reasonable way.

Not long ago a cross-country skier in Lake Placid, New York, stopped at a ranger station and asked directions to his lodge. The rangers advised him to take the shortest route because of the extreme cold. Later his wife and children called to report he had not arrived. The resulting search revealed the skier's body well off the route he had been advised to take. Apparently he had decided to take the scenic route instead.

Some people reject the advice of parents, friends, and counselors just because they want to do everything their own way. If you write out directions for them, they'll go a different way. If you tell them *Consumer Reports* rated a particular automobile tire or toaster or washing machine an exceptional value, they'll buy something else.

A woman I know threw away vacuum hose attachments and just used the hose. When her husband explained that the attachments were designed for specific cleaning purposes and to make the machine operate most effectively, she replied, "Oh, that's just a sales pitch. The way I use it is fine."

Advice from others, particularly unwanted advice, is often regarded as an insult or as a threat to individuality. But it's much more reasonable to view it as an opportunity to see things from a different perspective. There's no danger in considering advice carefully and weighing its merits. We've everything to gain and nothing to lose by taking that approach. If we find it wanting, we can reject it; if it proves sound, we can profit from it. The only investment we need to make is a little humility.

When Louise, a friend of mine, returned to work from vacation, the young worker who had covered for her gave her a long list of ways she had found to do the job better and more efficiently. Louise had to struggle mightily to resist dismissing the ideas. Her pride served up a variety of temptations: "She's too young to know anything; it's rude to tell others how to do their jobs; accepting her advice will be tantamount to admitting I haven't done my job right for all these years."

But the truth was the ideas were excellent. So she thanked the young woman and adopted the new approaches. By resisting false pride, Louise became a more effective worker. (Incidentally, the young woman's brilliance was recognized by all her superiors and she quickly rose to a position of responsibility and influence in the company.)

Good-Habit Builder

The next time someone offers you advice, suppress any irrational reaction you might have and give the advice thoughtful and fair-minded consideration. If it proves to be good advice, have the good sense to follow it.

10

Habits
for Good Relations
with Others

Despite our society's advances in science and technology, we have made little progress in basic human relations. Queries about how to get along with people,
particularly difficult people, are a staple of advice columns. And most of us have abundant evidence, some it
both personal and painful, that all is not well in many
modern relationships.

The divorce rate is almost 250 percent what it was
fifty years ago, and the solidity of many surviving marriages is more apparent than real. Young children are
often alienated from one or both parents, and the problem continues throughout their lives. Brothers and sisters refuse to speak to one another. And millions of
people have problems with in-laws, neighbors, clients,
customers, and co-workers.

At times we may be inclined to reason, I don't need
other people. If a relationship becomes troubled, I'll just
end it. But that is fallacious. We do need other people.
"No man is an island," wrote John Donne. And we cannot sever important relationships in life without wound-
ing ourselves. If our relations with others are not what

they should be, we should develop the habits that will improve them.

Expect More of Yourself Than of Others

There's nothing necessarily wrong with having expectations for others, particularly when we have responsibility for guiding them, as in the case of our children, or for supervising their work. The problem lies in expecting more of others than we do of ourselves. For some strange reason, that is often the case. How many times have you seen a parent berating a child for a fault you know the parent shares?

Such situations would be comical if they weren't so pathetic. The parent tells the child what to do and then promptly, continually, does the opposite. The child imitates the parent's behavior (a perfectly natural course of events—imitation is the way children learn). Then the parent becomes irate.

The problem isn't confined to parental relationships. Husbands and wives often are guilty of it, as are teachers and employers. And many a man has gotten angry over a neighbor's tardiness in returning a book when he himself never returns the neighbor's tools. Much of the frustration, complaining, and lingering bitterness people feel toward others, and toward the world in general, would be less acute if they concentrated on overcoming the very same faults in themselves.

Our expectations, like our attitudes, tend to show, whether we express them or not. The bad news is that setting high standards for others will often offend them. The good news is that setting high standards for ourselves will offend no one, and it may inspire others to set similar standards for themselves.

It follows, logically if paradoxically, that if we want to improve others, our best approach is to improve ourselves.

Good-Habit Builder

List the areas in which you have high expectations for others. Consider honestly whether you ask as much, if not more, of yourself. If you do not, formulate a higher standard and challenge yourself to meet it. Then adopt the motto, "Practicing high standards is more effective than merely preaching them."

Consider How You Displease Others

If you were asked to list the ways in which other people displease you, you'd probably run out of paper before you ran out of ideas. "My husband doesn't take the garbage out. He sits in front of the stupid screen watching men chase a ball around." Or "My wife doesn't know what punctuality means. And she wastes money on sale items we have no use for." And so on.

But what if, instead, you were asked to list the ways in which *you* displease others? Would you suffer an attack of amnesia? Or would your answers somehow turn into complaints? Wouldn't you say, for example, "My wife is bothered by my watching ball games, but she has no appreciation of sports."

Although it's undeniably unpleasant to identify our own faults, doing so is one of the best ways to improve our relations with others. Here are some starter questions to consider.

Are you reliable? Do you keep your word?
Do you shirk your obligations?
Are you punctual?
Are you overly talkative? Or are you uncommunicative?
Do you nag others? Are you a pest?
Are you sympathetic? Compassionate?
Are you forgetful?
Are you domineering?

Are you neighborly?
Do you have a positive outlook?
Are you intolerant or prejudiced toward any group?
Do you respect others' rights?
Are you responsible in financial matters?

Don't confine your answers to a simple yes or no. Think of examples of behavior that support your answers, and be sure they're typical. (Thinking of an *exception* to your usual behavior doesn't qualify.) In addition, consider the implications of your answers. If you are forgetful in certain circumstances, for example, ask what that suggests about you. Forgetting about eating or sleeping or doing something you really want to do probably means you are a serious person who becomes engrossed in your work. But forgetting promises to others or obligations suggests you are self-centered and insensitive to others.

As you answer these and other appropriate questions, remember that your goal is to penetrate your defensiveness and learn more about yourself, not to practice self-deception.

Good-Habit Builder

Each day for the next week, select one thing you do that displeases someone else and make a special effort to avoid doing it.

Postpone Speaking When Upset

A cartoon depicts two people sitting at a table. One looks at the other and says, "Why am I raising my voice? Because I'm *wrong.*" It is amusing because it expresses a truth that's seldom expressed. We do tend to raise our voices when we're wrong, no doubt to maintain the self-deception that we are right. But we hate to acknowledge, even to ourselves, that we do.

Anger, frustration, and other negative emotions bring out the worst in us. When we are in their grip, we seldom have our wits about us. Rationality flies and we become intemperate. If we feel offended, we respond in kind and become offensive. Something inside us says, "Use words as a weapon. Say something nasty, cruel, hurtful." So we say things we don't really mean, or things we do mean but have no business saying. We resurrect old issues that, rather than alleviating the present problem, compound it.

The wounds our words create at such times often go deep and leave lasting scars. Many an adult remembers an occasion almost half a century ago when, in a moment of rage, a parent said, "You're stupid!" or "I can never trust you not to make a mess of things!" It doesn't matter if the words were empty and in no way matched the parent's true feelings. They remain etched in memory and, if numerous enough, can cause divisions that never heal.

The saddest part is that these injuries are avoidable. All we need do is develop the habit of being silent at such inflammatory moments or, if that is too difficult, simply say, "I'm very upset and I know if I don't control myself, I'm apt to say something stupid I don't even mean. I care too much about our relationship to let that happen."

This act of self-control in no way denies that issues shouldn't be dealt with directly. It isn't the same as avoiding discussion. It merely postpones discussion until there is a better chance of its being positive and productive. By giving yourself time to calm down, sort out your feelings, and decide what you really want your reaction to be, you ensure that your better, more reasonable, and caring self will take command.

Good-Habit Builder

Make a special effort today to be aware of your emotions. Each time you realize that you are upset about something, remind yourself of your intention to postpone speaking. The urge to speak may be strongest then, so you will have to exercise unusual self-control the first few times. But after that, you'll find it much easier.

Apologize When You've Offended

One of the least remarked differences between old films of the 1930s, 1940s, and 1950s and modern ones is that today's films contain few scenes of reconciliation. One problem, of course, is that fewer characters in today's movies escape decapitation, combustion, or disembowelment. Another is that apologizing is frowned upon today, undoubtedly because it's associated with humility and therefore regarded as a threat to self-esteem. In the movies, and more importantly in real life, many people avoid apologizing. When they've offended someone, they just resume the relationship as if nothing had happened.

This isn't good enough. When we don't apologize, memory begins the process of self-serving and we run the risk not only of hurting others but also of hating them. As the Roman historian Tacitus observed nineteen hundred years ago, "It is human nature to hate those [we] have wronged." Worse, not apologizing can lead us to believe we are never at fault.

Is it easy to apologize? Not at all. But it is vitally important that we do so. The wronged person needs it in order to forgive us. We need it to affirm that we are not at the mercy of our conditioning, but in control of ourselves and responsible for what we say and do. Asking others' forgiveness restores our self-respect, relieves us of the burden of guilt, and enables us to forgive ourselves and renew our commitment to the relationship.

To frame your apologies, put yourself in the other person's place. See the situation from his or her perspective as well as your own. This will help you avoid being subjective and self-serving. Decide how much of the blame is yours; if you err, do so on the side of generosity rather than pride. Decide whether to say "I'm sorry it happened," "I'm sorry I overreacted," "I'm sorry for my part in it," or "I'm totally at fault and ask your forgiveness."

Good-Habit Builder

Think of a recent unpleasant incident that injured your relationship with someone. Ponder what happened and decide what form of apology is appropriate for you to make. Then make it straightforwardly and sincerely. And don't add any qualifications; in other words, don't say, "I was wrong, but so were you." Leave it to the other person's conscience to recommend that admission. And don't be bothered if it doesn't come at once.

Compliment Others

Think of a time when someone complimented you at just the right time, perhaps when you were feeling low and really needed a lift. Remember how you felt at that moment, how for at least a moment you forgot your troubles, your smile returned, and your step quickened? You can make others feel that same way too and simultaneously strengthen the bond you have with them.

Some people give compliments freely and naturally, even to strangers. (I'm referring to sincere people, not the slick salespeople who want to prepare us for major surgery on our wallets.) It's not surprising that these people are usually well liked.

Undoubtedly complimenting comes more easily to some than to others, but anyone can learn the knack. All it takes is practice. Begin by being more observant. Notice people's clothes, grooming, possessions, and personal characteristics, including the way they treat others. When you see something you like, express your reaction as a compliment. "I like your new hairdo"; "Is that a new car? You must be proud of it, it's very attractive"; "You were unbelievably patient with that clerk in the store"; "Your baby is beautiful."

Not long ago, I was waiting to board a plane and noticed a young couple with four children, the oldest about six. Waiting can be torture for little ones, I thought, but these children were so well-behaved, their parents obviously had taught them well. The thought had the potential to do good, but it could only realize that potential by being expressed.

"Excuse me," I said to the parents, "but I want to compliment you on how well-behaved your children are. You obviously work hard at being good parents." They beamed. And the children had a chance to hear a stranger reinforce the lessons they learned at home.

Good-Habit Builder

Begin taking closer notice of things you can compliment people about. Whenever you find something, express your reaction.

Be Tactful

Maureen always looked much younger than her age, but at age forty she came down with a serious illness. A year later she had conquered it but still felt and looked haggard. While shopping, she met Beth, whom she hadn't seen in a few years. "Maureen," Beth said, "I haven't seen you in years. I'm glad you finally look your age." Maureen was crushed.

Even if we assume, in charity, that Beth didn't know of Maureen's illness, her remark was stupid and cruel. She should have realized that when people look haggard there's usually a reason, and calling attention to some-one's appearance at such a time is, at best, insulting.

Unfortunately, such tactlessness is not uncommon. People ask childless couples, "Don't you want chil-dren?" only to find that the couple have tried unsuccess-fully for years. They ask, "Are you lonely at holiday times?" to a man whose wife died less than a year ago; "Do you ever hear from Mike?" to the ex-wife Mike abandoned for a younger woman; "Is it true that your brother's death was a suicide?" to someone in mourning; and "Oh, what a terrible scar to have on your face," to someone recovering from an automobile accident.

Even if you are seldom guilty of such obvious tactless-ness, like most people you probably are an occasional sufferer from "foot-in-mouth disease." The most com-mon cause is blurting out before thinking, and the best preventive is the reflective pause. Before you ask a ques-tion or make a statement about any matter that could be considered personal, ask yourself, "Is it tactful to ex-press what I have in mind?" If there is the slightest rea-son to believe the answer is no, remain silent. If some reaction is demanded, such as in encountering a grieving widow at a wake, just grasp her hand and say "I'm very sorry" or put your arm around her, squeeze her gently, and say nothing.

Good-Habit Builder

Recall one or more occasions where you said the wrong thing. Decide what you would say or do if a similar situa-tion arose today.

Express Gratitude

When Jesus was traveling to Jerusalem, he met ten lep-ers who greeted him. "Jesus! Master! Take pity on us." He told them to go and show themselves to the priests, and as they went they were cleansed. One of them, a Samaritan, turned back, praised God loudly, and threw himself at Jesus' feet in gratitude. And Jesus said, "Were not all ten made clean? But the other nine, where are they? Was no one found who turned back to give glory to God except this foreigner?" (Luke 17:13–18, JB).

Lack of gratitude is not new. And if people can be ungrateful to God, it's hardly surprising that they are ungrateful to one another. I feel more than a twinge of guilt in writing these words. I can think of so many people who were kind to me in my life, many of whom I never thought to thank. Two employers I worked for as a teenager, who by evaluating my work more generously than accurately made me feel competent and appreciated. Teachers in high school who were patient with my immaturity and laughed at my foolish jokes when they could have punished me. The college English instructor who inspired me to aim for excellence in writing and speaking. The graduate school professors whose dedication to teaching inspired my own teaching career. The many caring friends.

Perhaps my brief list has helped you recall some of the people to whom *you* own a debt of gratitude. That is the first step in developing the habit of expressing gratitude. The second is to seek those people out and thank them, however belatedly. A simple card will suffice, and sending it will be a wonderful blessing to them and to you.

Consider, first, your parents. A friend of mine recently received a completely unexpected letter from her twenty-seven-year-old married daughter, thanking her for all the years of loving, caring, and trying so hard to be a good mother to her children. My friend said it was impossible for her to express what a moving experience receiving that letter was.

But what of those who have died or can't be located? And what of the many strangers whose names you don't even know, men and women who extended themselves to you when they didn't have to, who did you a kindness merely for the sake of doing so? How can you show gratitude to these people? Not by words certainly, but by going out of your way to be kind to others, and doing it in memory of them.

Good-Habit Builder

Begin each day, for the next few days, with a reminder to express your gratitude to the many people who have brightened your life. Look for opportunities to help others. And when you find them, even if they are as small as holding the door for someone or letting someone ahead of you in the supermarket checkout line, do them cheerfully.

Show Affection and Love

Norman had been my neighbor for more than seven years, a gentle person, always ready to help when needed, respected by everyone on the block. Now he was gone, the victim of a sudden heart attack, and family and friends were gathered in the funeral chapel to pay our respects.

Norman's three children, whose ages ranged from late twenties to mid thirties, had flown in as soon as they'd gotten the news. They were all successful in their careers, and Norman had been proud of them. Whenever he received a letter or a phone call, he'd be beaming for days. Their communication, however, was infrequent. Like so many people today, their lives were hectic and they never seemed to find time to write or call.

They were shaken by his untimely death. Emily, the oldest, was remorseful. "If only I'd known," she told me. "I planned to spend the holidays with him this year. I've neglected our relationship. I thought I'd have time. But now— " She turned away in tears.

Norman, Jr., confided that he had looked up to his father more than to any other person. "I loved him so much," he explained, "but you know, I could never bring myself to tell him. After Mom died, I vowed I would, but I kept avoiding it. I never once in all those years let him know what was in my heart."

The story touched me because it made me remember my relationship with my own father. He never said he loved me and was proud of me. I knew he did only because other people told me: "Your father is so proud of you—he's always talking about you, extolling your achievements."

I felt that way about him too. I can still recall how powerful the emotion was when I was a child. One occasion is still vivid in my memory almost half a century later.

We were spending an evening with his partner's family. My father was playing the violin, his partner the harmonica, and his partner's wife the piano. Their daughter and I were singing the old ballad, "Always": "I'll be loving you, always. . . . " I looked at my father and thought, "I love you so very much, Dad." I tried to continue singing, but my voice broke and tears welled in my eyes. To cover my embarrassment, I pretended to cough.

More than thirty years passed before I could say those words to him. And even then I expressed them in a letter rather than in person.

Why are negative emotions so easy to voice and positive ones so difficult? We complain, criticize, reproach, and denounce without hesitation, even when our words wound others. But for some reason we cannot bring ourselves to express warm, healing thoughts. Perhaps, for men at least, expressions of affection and love seem to imply weakness. Perhaps we lack the humility required to expose our vulnerability.

If you would find it difficult to look someone in the

eye and say, "Your friendship means a great deal to me," then invest a little imagination and find a way to convey the thought indirectly. A woman I know clips little items from the many magazines she subscribes to and sends them to her close friends. On one occasion she sent an article about a movie star she and her friend admired as teenagers, a picture she took on a visit to their hometown, and some pictures and an article about miniature horses (her friend was a collector). Even though the accompanying letter was brief and matter-of-fact, the clippings conveyed a message of affection. They said, I think about you often and remember things we shared.

The rewards of expressing affection and love outweigh any initial awkwardness we might feel. We give others the delight of knowing that they are cherished. We buttress our relationships to better endure moments of strain. We experience the incomparable satisfaction of bringing joy to those we love. And we spare ourselves the pain of realizing, at some future mourning time, that the opportunity to share our deepest feelings has been forever lost.

Good-Habit Builder

List the people for whom you feel deep affection. Consider your parents, spouse, children, other relatives, and friends. Next to each name write what you most admire and appreciate about that person. Then when you see each of these people again, communicate your feelings. Do it face to face, if possible. Put your arm around the person, look him or her in the eye, and speak simply and directly.

"Joan, I want you to know you're the best friend I've ever had; you're always there when I need you" or "Paul, I often thank God for you—you're the best son a father could have." If you can't bring yourself to express your feelings this way, find an indirect way of doing so.

Be Pleasant

It is said that the face people have after fifty is the face they deserve. Look around you. Some people look youthful even into their eighties (and without face lifts and other desperate measures). The genes have something to do with how the years treat us, to be sure, but so does our manner toward others.

The three of us were in the elevator. It was a beautiful Florida day, bright and sunny and not too humid. Barbara and I spoke to the woman. "What a lovely day," we said and smiled. She frowned and replied, "It'll get hot and humid before long, though, and I hate that weather." As we exited, Barbara whispered to me, "Some people would complain about being *rich!*"

Gravity ultimately has its way with our bodies, making muscles droop and sag. At best we are involved in a holding action against its ravages. But there is one set of muscles we need never surrender to gravity, the ones that surround our mouths and enable us to smile. And those have a magical effect on the muscles in our brow. (If you doubt this, try to smile with your mouth and frown with your brow at the same time.)

In *Making Contact*, Arthur Wassmer says that when you want to let people know you are relaxed with them and feel comfortable and friendly toward them, use the SOFTEN approach. In other words, Smile, have an Open posture, lean Forward, Touch them, maintain Eye contact, and Nod when you agree with them. Such behavior, notes Alan Garner, author of *Conversationally Speaking*, not only pleases others, it makes us feel better too. "When you express an emotion outwardly," he writes, "you will tend to experience it inwardly."

So smile at others. And while you're at it, make an effort to speak pleasant thoughts. This doesn't mean being a Polyanna. If unpleasant messages need to be communicated, so be it. But don't go out of your way to be the bearer of bad tidings. And never take a negative view when an equally good case can be made for the positive view. You'll soon find that people find it more enjoyable to be with you. In fact, you'll probably find it more enjoyable being with yourself.

Good-Habit Builder

Go through an entire day stressing the positive. Smile and speak pleasantly to people. Don't worry if some of them don't smile back or if what you say seems innocuous, like "Wonderful weather we're having" or even "Have a nice day." With a little practice, you'll think of more original or meaningful comments.

Receive Criticism Graciously

The book of Proverbs (20:19, KJV) counsels, "Meddle not with him that flattereth with his lips." And sages have long echoed that counsel. Writes Jonathan Swift, "'Tis an old maxim in the schools,/ That flattery's the food of fools." Sir Richard Steele adds, "Among all the diseases of the mind there is not one more epidemical or more pernicious than the love of flattery." And Molière advises, "The more we love our friends, the less we flatter them."

Wisdom notwithstanding, it's a rare person who does not prefer flattery to criticism. When we are offered a compliment, even one that is patently unjustified, we have difficulty reacting reasonably and wondering, "Can this person's judgment really be so deficient or am I being set up for something, a loan perhaps?" Conversely, when someone criticizes us, our urge is strong to dismiss the idea as unworthy and resent the speaker for proposing it.

Few efforts are more vital for good relations with others and for self-improvement than the effort to overcome this irrationality and appreciate other people's criticism. Those who criticize are doing us a favor by providing a perspective different from our own, showing us how the world may see us, prompting us to overcome our weaknesses.

But what of those cases where their motives in criticizing are less than honorable, where they are envious of us and want to plant seeds of self-doubt? Such cases do occur, though surely less frequently than we pretend. Does it make sense to say that these people are also doing us a favor? Yes. At the very least, they offer us an opportunity to practice humility.

Receiving criticism graciously doesn't mean endorsing what is said. It merely means accepting it, without taking offense, and evaluating it objectively. It may or may not prove insightful; that is for us to decide on reflection. But we should not resent the person who offers it. In doing so, he or she may very well have proven to be a friend.

Good-Habit Builder

The next time someone criticizes you, say, "I realize it takes courage to criticize people and run the risk of displeasing them. I want you to know that I appreciate your caring enough for me to run that risk." And keep that thought in mind as you evaluate the criticism.

Resist Giving Advice

The temptation to give unasked-for advice remains strong, even increases, with advancing age. Grandparents, for example, often feel an overpowering urge to advise their children on the art of parenting. After all, they know more than their children about the subject; they've been through it all, so what could be more sensible, more caring, than helping them make the right decisions and avoid making mistakes?

Or so it seems. But it's a dangerous business. For one thing, grown children usually feel a little insecure and therefore defensive, because the challenge of parenting is relatively new to them and they aren't sure they're entirely equal to it. For another, they may be harboring resentment about their own upbringing that needs only a trigger mechanism, such as a parent volunteering unasked-for advice, to be released.

If the wisest policy on unasked-for advice is "Butt out," what's the wisest advice on asked-for advice? Exactly the same, for pretty much the same reason. Asking for advice does signify a desire, but it's seldom a desire for advice. Rather, as John Steinbeck observed, it's a desire for corroboration. By the time people seek counsel from others, they usually struggle with their problem, make assumptions, form opinions, and in some cases reach a final decision. Thus, without being fully aware of the fact, they are looking to have us guess their thoughts and validate them. Even if they assure us, "I really want your view of this; don't hold back; be totally honest with me," they may really want only our approval.

Suppose a friend approaches you and says, "I'm so confused. I love my boyfriend, but he's thoughtless and insensitive and has a violent temper. Do you think I should break up with him?" You may want to say, "Absolutely. That's not the kind of man that makes a good husband or father. You're better off without him." But your friend may have already decided that love conquers all and is expecting you to agree. By speaking your mind you may lose her friendship.

In such a situation, there's little chance of winning. That's why the best approach is, wherever possible, to resist giving advice, at least until you have probed the other person's thinking. In the case of the woman with the thoughtless boyfriend you might say, "Your decision will be a tough one to make, I know. You must have agonized over it. Would you care to share your thinking with me?" Her answer will probably reveal whether she has already decided or whether she is open to suggestion.

No matter how cautious you are, there will still be situations in which you decide that friendship requires you to speak your mind or where it is clear that, though you *may* be resented for speaking, you will *definitely* be resented for not speaking. In those cases, remember Samuel Taylor Coleridge's thought: "Advice is like snow; the softer it falls, the longer it dwells upon, and the deeper it sinks into the mind." Speak moderately, and add the disclaimer, "I'm honored that you've asked me, but I hope you consult with others as well, because I wouldn't want my advice to prove unwise and hurt you."

Good-Habit Builder

The next time you feel the urge to offer someone unasked-for advice, stifle that urge. The next time you are asked for advice, first probe to find out whether the person really wants your honest opinion. Then, if you decide to give it, add an appropriate disclaimer.

Avoid Boasting

Boasting comes in either of two forms, proclamations of past accomplishments or predictions of future ones. The former announce, I have an inflated sense of my own importance and a corresponding insensitivity to the feelings of those around me; I love to bore people. The latter create an unnecessary burden of performance that, ironically, often *causes* failure. In addition, they set in motion a downward spiral to embarrassment, face-saving, more boasting, further embarrassment, and so on, ensuring that the boaster's last state will always be worse than the first.

Here is a comparison of that downward spiral with the more favorable progression possible by embracing modesty and humility.

The Boastful Person	The Unboastful Person
Predicts great success, trumpets skills, etc.	Says nothing about chances for success. If asked, merely says, "I'll try my best."
When successful, receives no congratulations from others because busy with self-congratulation.	When successful, impresses others by having been so modest about chances.
When failing, is embarrassed and so is likely to make excuses, save face by charging "foul," deceive himself or herself.	When failing, is disappointed but suffers little loss of face because no predictions of success were made.
Being dishonest with self, denies having made any mistake, so no lesson is learned from the experience.	Being honest with self, is open to acknowledge whatever mistakes may have been made and to correct them.
Is tempted to meet subsequent challenges with increased boasting, thus decreasing future chances of success.	By accurate self-assessment, increases chances of success in the future.

Since it's possible to boast without realizing it, it does little good to ask yourself, "Are there any situations in which I tend to be boastful?" Instead, you'll have to monitor your conversations and be alert for instances of boasting.

Good-Habit Builder

For the next several days be alert for situations in which you are tempted to dwell on your past accomplishments or to predict future successes. Resist the temptation. Let others praise what you have done. (If they don't, conclude that those accomplishments are best left unreported.) Describe your present and future endeavors, if you wish, but offer no predictions about their outcome.

11

Habits for Satisfaction in Life

Bustling activity, much clowning and laughing, pats on the back and warm hugs, a mingling of music, shrieks of recognition, and animated conversation—the whole scene positively oozes with camaraderie and good cheer. We see it dozens of times a day on television commercials for beer and wine coolers. And then there are the commercials for new cars and cruise lines, showing people driving scenic coastal highways and pastoral country roads or sunning-swimming-dancing-eating-embracing in breathtaking rapidity.

These and many other commercials have at least one thing in common: They depict life as an unbroken series of exciting and memorable moments. And television programs themselves reinforce the image. On game shows people squeal and jump up and down against a backdrop of brightly colored flashing lights. On Donohue, Oprah, and Geraldo a few dozen people make impassioned statements in rapid succession. On the soaps and dramatic programs, quick cuts among multiple stories create an artificially rapid pace (so viewers won't lose patience and change channels). And on the news, machine-gun delivery gives us our daily ration of the world's joys and woes.

Television moguls may offer solemn assurances that such contrived excitement has no negative effect on viewers, but common sense says otherwise. Vicarious experience, like the real thing, shapes expectations, particularly those of the young. It's a good bet that twenty or so years from now a lavishly funded research study will conclude that much of children's disenchantment with school and their parents' unhappiness with marriage and parenthood and careers is attributable to the impossible expectations created by television.

Life just can't deliver proms, graduations, marriages, and family reunions every day. And despite the fast pace of modern living, birthdays still come only once a year. The festiveness of holidays and special celebrations is a wonderful blessing in life, something to be eagerly anticipated and savored, but not expected or sought or demanded all the time.

Fortunately, we don't need constant excitement to achieve satisfaction in life. We need only to cultivate a few simple habits.

Add Interest To Your Life

As Jacob M. Braude wisely observed, "All we need to make us really happy is something to be enthusiastic about." The problem is, it's impossible to become enthusiastic without first being interested, and the popular view of interest prevents that. We think of interest as a quality that resides in subjects: "This book is interesting"; "That discussion was fascinating." But that is a half-truth, at best. Admittedly, the way a subject is presented may be more or less lively. But that doesn't make the subject itself interesting or boring.

Everything in life is potentially fascinating or hopelessly boring, and the choice of which it will be is largely ours. In this sense we make life what it is for us. And this is no small matter. Whether we can't wait to get up out of bed in the morning and set about our day's activities or have to struggle; whether time passes quickly or drags painfully; whether we derive joy or only boredom from living; whether we remain active, alert, and exuberant as a small child throughout our years or shrivel up inside—all these are decisions we are free to make.

For many people, the grass always looks greener in the next stage of life. They suffer through school in the hope that graduating and getting a job will fulfill them. Then they find that they hate their jobs and suffer through with the idea that retirement will make them happy. Sad to say, if that is their attitude, retirement too will usually prove boring.

How foolish it is to wait for life to perform some magic when you alone have that power. One way to use it is to balance mental activities and physical activities. Many people lead completely sedentary lives. They sit at a desk all day and then go home to sit in front of the TV set all evening. Their exercise consists of walking to the car or the elevator. If that is the case with you, force yourself to do something physical every day. It doesn't have to be something strenuous, such as running, swimming laps, or playing tennis (though those activities are wonderful). Bicycling and walking are excellent aerobic activities.

On the other hand, if you already do a great deal of physical activity, add more mental activity to achieve a balance. Think of a subject you've dismissed as uninteresting and give it another chance—for example, furniture making, history, geography, botany, interior decorating, literature, art, or music. Get some books from the library or go to the theater or a museum. If you find the first subject doesn't appeal to you, try another and then another.

One way to combine the physical and the mental and add interest to your life is to travel. If you can afford to do so, take a trip. Consider leaving the car at home and taking a bus, train, or plane for a change of perspective. Begin with a short trip, preferably with a group and a tour guide, and take along a camera to record scenes of interest. Incidentally, becoming an amateur photographer will sharpen your eye for unusual scenes and stimulate your interest in people and places.

Don't make the mistake of assuming that you'll want to travel in retirement if you haven't traveled earlier. Too many people promise themselves they'll travel later in life, but when "later" comes, they no longer have the necessary energy or are fearful of straying far from home or their health won't permit it. Start traveling early, and you'll find it easier to travel later.

Good-Habit Builder

Is most of your everyday activity mental or physical? If it is mental, make a list of physical activities that will achieve a better balance and make your life more interesting. If it is physical, make a list of mental activities. Begin pursuing at least one of those activities today.

Avoid Being Self-Absorbed

When Lou Carp was eighty-nine years old he devoted two to three days a week to Goldwater Memorial Hospital's disabled patients in New York. To get there he had to take the subway and a bus. He read to the patients, told funny stores, gave them candy and pens, and made telephone calls for them. When asked why he did it, he said, "Man is not built just for himself."

The president of APA Transport, a trucking company, celebrated the firm's thirty-fifth anniversary by sending every worker in the company, from vice-president to janitor, on either a three-day cruise on the *Queen Elizabeth II* or for a weekend in Las Vegas. Part-time employees were included, as were all spouses. This generosity cost him over $1 million.

For over twenty-one years Dorothy Dixon, of Fort Lauderdale, Florida, provided shelter for abandoned, abused, or neglected youngsters. In all, she helped more than fourteen hundred kids. When people comment on the contribution she has made, she says she received much more than she gave.

These admirable people have at least one thing in common, the ability to see beyond self-interest and be concerned about others. You may not have heard about them, or about thousands like them, because if their stories are told at all, they are buried in the lower right-hand corner of page 28 of your newspaper. (Doesn't it seem that, as bad news keeps increasing, at some point it should become less newsworthy and surrender the front page to good news?)

It's not fashionable today to be an altruist. ME-ism is a jealous perspective and allows little thought of others. Celebrities fill the airwaves with talk of "*my* new film," "*my* record," "*my* autobiography," and "*my* sacred opinions on everything." And many other people are preoccupied with *my* pain, *my* love life, *my* belongings, *my* work, *my* achievements, *my* disappointments, *my* hopes, *my* plans, *my* ego.

Our age has forgotten what our less educated, less sophisticated grandparents knew well: Self-absorption is a curse. The more lightly we carry ourselves, the less our burden. The moment we unwrap our minds from ourselves, our misfortunes seem less tragic, offenses committed against us less heinous. Think about it. If someone cuts you off on the highway or lets her dog defecate on your lawn, which attitude will produce less anxiety: "What a rude thing to do!" or "That so-and-so offended me. *Me,* can you believe it? *Me!*"

The antidote to self-absorption is concern for other people. Try going through an entire day without thinking about yourself. Focus on other people, those around you or those you read about in the newspaper. For example, find a story about a selfless act. Let your mind linger in admiration. If you can find the selfless person's address, write a letter of praise. If you can't, clip the article and send it to someone you know who'd be uplifted by it.

If you know someone who has lost a loved one or suffered a serious disappointment, imagine what he or she is feeling; share the feeling, and then consider what you might say or do to alleviate it or help the person deal with it.

If you have fallen into the habit of thinking too much about yourself, you'll find this activity refreshing. In addition, you may develop new friendships. As Charles L. Allen sagely observes, "You can make more friends in a month by being interested in them than in ten years by trying to get them interested in you."

Good-Habit Builder

Begin today to think about others more than yourself. Whenever you find your thoughts focusing on yourself (your health, your financial situation, your popularity, and so on), turn them to the people around you at that moment or to those who have a special place in your life. When you are conversing with other people, speak less and listen more.

Have a Positive Outlook

The story is told of the wicked baron who hated a cobbler for his cheerfulness. The cobbler would sing all day long while mending shoes. The baron had him thrown into prison, but the man continued to sing, saying, "I'm delighted not to have any work to do." Then the baron sent him into the castle yard to chop wood. Still he sang cheerfully, thinking, What a marvelous opportunity to get exercise! Finally, the baron had him confined in a dank dungeon. Still he sang, saying, "What a marvelous place to reflect on God's goodness without distraction." The baron, it is said, had a seizure and died and the cobbler went back to his shop, where he sang as before.

An improbable tale, of course. No sane person would be quite that cheerful in the face of such adversity. But, then, not many people face such adversity. The lesson is really about our potential for a positive attitude in less dramatic circumstances. Given the number of people who hate their jobs, the millions of tranquilizers sold each year, and the moaning and groaning we hear from those around us when minor difficulties arise, the lesson is apt.

It wouldn't matter much *how* we responded to everyday challenges if our overall outlook didn't depend on our reactions. But it does. "When you look at the world in a narrow way," Horace Rutledge writes, "how narrow it seems! When you look at it in a mean way, how mean it is! When you look at it selfishly, how selfish it is! But when you look at it in a broad, generous, friendly spirit, what wonderful people you find in it."

Naturally, it's much easier to start the day with a positive attitude than to maintain that attitude as difficulties arise, so set yourself the more demanding challenge by making three resolutions.

Whenever you are forced to change your plans, do so gracefully, without becoming distraught, blaming anyone, or displaying signs of immaturity. Invest any negative energy you may feel into the positive task of making new plans.

Try to make inconvenience an opportunity. If your car breaks down and you have to walk, don't trudge and grumble; walk briskly and enjoy the exercise. If the television set breaks while you are watching it, don't curse your luck; take the opportunity to play with the children or talk to your spouse.

Take life a little less seriously. When you are about to become angry or anxious, step back from the situation and try to find something humorous in it. If you succeed, take the time to enjoy a good laugh. This is not frivolous advice; more and more doctors are confirming that the ability to laugh is good medicine. And it is probably most potent when we are laughing at ourselves.

Good-Habit Builder

Carry out your resolutions today. At the end of the day, appraise your progress. If it falls short of reasonable expectations, redouble your effort tomorrow.

Make Someone Close to You Happy

Many a man will enter the neighborhood bar, pat everyone on the back, buy his cronies a drink, and engage in a couple of hours of friendly banter. Then he'll go home and mumble a greeting to his wife, complain about the evening meal, and tell the children he is too tired to play with them. Many a woman who is sweet and kind and thoughtful in the office is transformed into a shrew when she goes home at night. And many children who would go to any length not to offend their peers spew vile, hateful words at their parents.

Few of us, let's hope, are that bad. Still, most of us tend to reserve our worst treatment for those nearest and dearest to us. It's as if we have a NICE mask that we put on when we leave the house in the morning and hang up when we return. What an absurd business! If we have to mistreat some people (and, happily, we don't), why in the name of logic don't we choose those who mean the least to us?

The problem may be simple carelessness: monitoring our behavior while with outsiders, relaxing our vigilance at home. If this is the case, the solution is equally simple: Adjust your priorities. Be on your very best behavior at home. One strategy is to observe appropriate DON'TS: "Don't raise your voice," "Don't neglect the common courtesies, such as saying 'Please' and 'Thank you,' " and so on. But a more important one is to observe appropriate DOS. Here are just a few:

Perform some helpful act that is not required of you, at least once a day. (Assigned chores don't count.)

Do something with your loved one, at least several times a week, more often if possible, that he or she wants to do but you don't. If you must make a sacrifice to do it, so much the better. But be sure to do it with a generous spirit. (No sulking or playing the martyr.)

Say something kind, encouraging, or complimentary to each of your loved ones every day. If some of them live elsewhere, call them at least once a week and find a way to work the uplifting comment into the conversation.

The last suggestion brings to mind a neighbor of mine who lost his wife not long ago. They had been married for more than fifty years. When I expressed my sympathy to him, he said, "She was a wonderful woman and I miss her terribly. But I'm happy about one thing—I always shared my feelings with her. At least once a day, every day of our life together, I told her I loved her."

Good-Habit Builder

Think of as many specific ways as you can to make those close to you happy. Put at least one of them into practice today.

Do a Kindness for Someone Who Can't Repay

Edward Anderson had been a minister in the north-eastern United States for almost sixty years when he retired at age eighty-four. Wanting to remain active, he decided to combine his training in religious counseling with his hobby of watercolor painting. On postcards, he created delicate pictures of birds, flowers, butterflies, and miniature landscapes. No two were quite the same, but each included a special message of hope.

He sent these cards not to friends, relatives, or influential people but to lonely invalids who had little to brighten their lives and could do nothing for him in return. Each person on his list received a card once a week. This work of kindness he continued every day for three years. He was working on a postcard when he died at eighty-seven.

Doing a kindness for anyone is praiseworthy, but when the person is someone who can return it—an employer, say, or someone else we can profit by impressing—the satisfaction we enjoy can be diminished by our hope of gain. But when the person can't repay us, our satisfaction is deepened, especially when we act in secret, for then we know we are truly acting in charity.

Kindness is always a kind of giving, but there are many ways to give. We may contribute money to the various funds that support needy children in poor countries of the world or to organizations that feed the hungry and heal the sick or minister to the needs of the neglected, the shut in, or the disenfranchised.

We may contribute our expertise, as lawyers do when they provide free legal counsel to those who cannot afford to pay. I know two physicians and their nurse wives who for many years took a three-month annual leave from their comfortable practices and traveled to Africa to provide medical care in jungle clinics.

Those who cannot afford to give money and have no

special professional expertise to offer can give something equally valuable and needed, their time. Gail and
John Wessells of Greene, New York, spend two days
each week visiting the most neglected of medical patients, those with serious brain injuries. Some are cata-
tonic or otherwise unable to communicate, even by
raising an eyebrow; others are minimally functional. Gail
and John read the Bible to them, sing songs for them,
and keep them company.

Whether your gift is money, expertise, time, a simple
smile of brotherhood, or a kind word of encouragement,
you will be well rewarded—and not merely in satisfaction. The exercise of humanity makes us more fully
human.

Good-Habit Builder

For the next day or two look around you for opportunities to do kindnesses to those who cannot repay you.
Consider opportunities that exist in your community or
outside it, at your place of work, or in your daily travels
to and from work. Consider the kindnesses you might do
in each situation. Then do one or more. If you are able
to do a particular kindness regularly, so much the better.

Expect the Best of People

Aesop, the story goes, was once seated by a road and a
man came by and inquired what sort of people lived in
Athens. Aesop replied, "First tell me where you are
from and the kind of people who live there."

The man frowned and said, "I come from Argos, and
the people there are a terrible bunch—liars, crooks, and
troublemakers. I'm glad to be leaving there."

"I'm sorry to say you'll find the people of Athens
much the same as those you described," Aesop said.

Later another traveler came by and asked Aesop the same question. Aesop again said, "First tell me where you are from and describe the people there."

The man brightened and replied, "I come from Argos, and the people there are friendly, good-hearted, and decent."

"I'm happy to say you'll find the people of Athens much the same," Aesop told him.

The moral is that our expectations tend to be self-fulfilling. People's performance will often rise, or sink, to match our prior assessment. Lack of faith in a person, particularly a child, can destroy self-confidence and effectively block him or her from achieving competency. On the other hand, many a parent has found that trusting a child can create a trustworthy child. And many an optimistic teacher has drawn talent from a student who, in the view of others, possessed none.

Naturally, our confidence may not be sufficient to overcome all the previous experiences of the person's life. Prudence suggests we not walk through a gang-ruled, crime-ridden neighborhood at night. And we should be ready for a certain amount of disappointment if people don't measure up to expectations.

Nevertheless, the satisfaction we derive from being able to say, "I was right in thinking the best of this person," outweighs the sorrow of the occasional "I was wrong." And in the latter situations, we still have the consolation of having taken the chance and believed in people.

Good-Habit Builder

Consider the various situations in which you have a choice between expecting the best of people and expecting less than that. In the days and weeks ahead, whenever possible, expect the best.

Distinguish Between Wants and Needs

"In the affluent society," writes economist John Kenneth Galbraith, "no useful distinction can be made between luxuries and necessaries [sic]." Though he didn't intend it as such, this would serve as an appropriate motto for modern advertising. Every product, every service, is presented to us not as an answer to our desires but as the fulfillment of our deepest human needs. When children plead "Oh, I really n-e-e-d it, I just h-a-v-e to have it," they are echoing this refrain.

Popular culture promotes the equation "Happiness equals having sufficient money to buy all the material things you desire." It holds up for our admiration the glitterati of the society, conspicuous consumers, the "rich and famous." Since few can hope to copy their lifestyles, most are left to envy them. Edward Arlington Robinson underlined the folly of such envy in his well-known poem, "Richard Cory":

> Whenever Richard Cory went down town,
> We people on the pavement looked at him:
> He was a gentleman from sole to crown,
> Clean favored, and imperially slim.
>
> And he was always quietly arrayed,
> And he was always human when he talked;
> But still he fluttered pulses when he said,
> "Good morning," and he glittered when he walked.
>
> And he was rich—yes, richer than a king—
> And admirably schooled in every grace;
> In fine, we thought that he was everything
> To make us wish that we were in his place.
>
> So on we worked, and waited for the light,
> And went without the meat and cursed the bread;
> And Richard Cory, one calm summer night,
> Went home and put a bullet in his head.

Galbraith and advertisers notwithstanding, there has always been and always will be a vital distinction between luxuries and necessities, wants and needs. And since our affluent, materialistic society tends to blur that distinction, we should be conscientious about clarifying it. The basic physical necessities are food, shelter, and clothing. The special circumstances of our lives may also create other needs, such as provision for illness, tools for our work, and transportation. At least as important as physical necessities are intellectual and spiritual ones, including communication skills, knowledge, wisdom, self-discipline, and a sense of right and wrong.

Gourmet food, palatial estates, exotic furs, state-of-the-art tools, and fine motorcars, however, are not necessities but luxuries, no matter how much we may want them or, in the case of the rich, have become accustomed to them. The same is true for most of what is advertised in newspapers and magazines and on radio and television.

To be satisfied with our lives, we need to separate our wants from our needs, control our desire for material things, and make a firm commitment to meet our intellectual and spiritual needs.

Good-Habit Builder

Consider all the things you have recently thought about having. List each as either NEEDS or WANTS. Decide whether each listing is physical, intellectual, or spiritual. Extend the list to include things you haven't thought of recently but deserve inclusion. Review your final list and determine the order of importance.

Remind Yourself, *Noblesse Oblige*

As Brad pulls out of his driveway on his way to work, he has that wonderful "This is going to be a great day" feeling. The radio is playing an upbeat tune, and he whistles in accompaniment.

A few minutes later he's on the interstate. Suddenly a car speeds up on his right. When the driver is barely past, he swerves into Brad's lane, forcing him to jam on the brakes and two or three drivers behind him to do likewise.

When fear subsides, anger takes over. "Crazy, inconsiderate slob," Brad mutters. A mile or so later, a line of cars is entering the freeway. The lead car is edging forward and signaling to turn in. Instead of letting it merge, Brad surges forward and says aloud, "Don't pull in on me, buddy."

Sound familiar? Similar situations occur all the time: at work, while shopping, at home. Someone behaves rudely to us and we let ourselves become infected by the rudeness. As a result we ruin our own day and often several other people's as well.

We don't see it that way, of course, and that's the problem. Instead of saying, "I am allowing my day to be ruined," we say, "That driver has ruined my day by upsetting me and causing me to lose my composure and mistreat others."

Other people can control our behavior only if we assent. The choice is ours. When others are rude, we can imitate them . . . or instead be courteous. When others indulge in gossip, we can join in . . . or remain silent. When others express negativism and pessimism, we can darken our view to match theirs . . . or we can be positive and optimistic.

Admittedly, it is not always easy to resist responding in kind, particularly when we have been personally offended. We need some way to remind ourselves to respond in a way we can be proud of later. The best way, I have found, is to repeat the French *"noblesse oblige,"* the literal translation of which is "nobility obligates." Here is the larger meaning:

"Someone has just behaved badly to me. I realize that because I know the right way to behave. Perhaps the other person lacks this understanding or lacks the self-discipline to apply it. In any case, my knowledge creates an obligation for me: Because I know better, I should do better. I will now react accordingly."

By repeating this phrase, we recall the thought it represents and are motivated to act better than we otherwise might.

Good-Habit Builder

Read the meaning of *noblesse oblige* several times, until you are sure you will remember it. Then, whenever someone does something that either offends you or tempts you to act against your principles (for example, by gossiping), repeat the phrase to yourself, recall the thought, and choose a reaction you will be proud of later.

Take Note of Your Improvement

If we're too close to something, we don't see it very clearly. Small changes can occur without our noticing. The best illustration of this is a child's growth. When aunts, uncles, or grandparents visit, they are able to see how much taller and filled out the child is, whereas the parents were not really aware of any change.

Your progress at self-improvement may be similarly difficult to see. From time to time you may get the impression that you are marking time, hopelessly bogged down in your efforts to improve. This feeling is undoubtedly aggravated by the prevailing notion that instant gratification is your birthright, so you may become depressed and give up trying precisely when you are beginning to make significant progress.

At such times you'll need to shift the focus of your self-examination from finding things you want to improve to identifying what you've *already* improved. This shift in no way contradicts the idea expressed through-out this book—that the modern emphasis on self-esteem can block self-improvement. The problem with this em-phasis is that it is wildly excessive. There's nothing wrong with taking stock of your accomplishments if you do so at the right time and for the right reason.

The right time is when weariness or depression threaten your sense of purpose. The right reason is to confirm that your efforts at self-improvement are really making a difference. Self-improvement is like mountain climbing. Our main focus should be upward on the chal-lenge before us, but now and then it's beneficial to stop for a moment, look back at the distance we've covered, and draw strength for the climb ahead.

Good-Habit Builder

The next time you begin to weary of the effort toward self-improvement, or feel that you are not making prog-ress, look back through this book at the sections you have already read and applied. Reflect on the ways you have already improved and take encouragement from them.

12

Habits
for Spirituality

Spirituality means an abiding relationship with God. The key word is "abiding." It is so easy to confine our dealings with God to times when we are in need. As long as our lives are going well, we may forget. Then suddenly, when misfortune comes, we rush to God in supplication. A sweetheart breaks our heart and we turn to God for consolation. We lose our job and we beg God's blessing on our efforts to find another. A loved one dies and we ask for comfort in our grief. We contract a serious disease and we plead for a miracle.

Such approaches to God qualify as a relationship, but not as an abiding one because they are inconstant, shallow, and self-serving. How would we feel if our children called or wrote only when they wanted to ask a favor? Probably more used than loved. Turning to God only in times of need is no different.

Genuine spirituality means keeping God present in our lives at all times: good times as well as bad, happy times as well as sad, in success as well as in failure. It doesn't require us to carry the Bible everywhere we go and limit conversation to the recitation of proverbs and parables. Those who do such things are not necessarily spiritual; conversely, many deeply spiritual people don't do them.

A spiritual person is one who is constantly aware of God's presence, and delights in it, and whose thoughts and words and actions reflect—openly or secretly—the desire to please God.

Seek Out and Cultivate Silence

If you've ever tried to attract birds, you know how difficult a task it is. They flutter away at the slightest movement, the faintest noise. If we want them to approach, we must remain perfectly still and exercise great patience. Perhaps there is more profound significance than we know in the fact that traditional Christian symbolism pictures the Holy Spirit as a dove.

As Martin Luther observed, God works "within us" but not "without us." And one of our most important tasks is to create a favorable atmosphere for spiritual growth. An essential element in that atmosphere is silence. Modern life, unfortunately, tends to fill every moment with noise. We rise to the sound of an alarm clock jangling or blaring music, turn on the television for the morning news, pop a cassette in our automobile's tape player as we drive to work. As our day proceeds, we talk to others or listen to the hum of computers or an assortment of whines, whizzes, clangs, honks, and buzzes. When we arrive home, we automatically turn on the television once again.

A quiet walk or jog in the park used to provide respite from noise and a chance to meditate. But the Walkman radio tempts us to fill even that time with noise.

God will not compete with cacophony, will not *capture* our attention; we must be freely give it. Like a dove, God's Holy Spirit approaches us and hovers, waiting for us to quiet the human sounds in our ears and in our hearts. Though it is possible to find what T. S. Eliot called "the still point of the turning world" within ourselves while remaining in the world's din, the task is much more manageable if we escape that din and its inevitable distraction.

Begin by choosing a time of day when you can be alone in a quiet place. Perhaps the best time will be late at night or early in the morning. Free yourself of activity and, if possible, eliminate all noise. Set aside all everyday concerns and open your mind and heart to God. In the beginning, you may find it helpful to hold one or more of the following questions in mind: Where am I now in my life? Where should I be? What does God want of me? How can I best use my talents for God's purposes? Hold these questions lightly, making no conscious effort to answer them, feeling no anxiety about them, just remaining open.

Stay in this meditation as long as you find it comfortable. That may be only a few minutes at first, but in time you may stay much longer. Don't expect to hear a loud voice or have visions. Much of the time you will experience nothing but silence. That in itself is therapeutic for the soul. But remain alert for the vague thoughts that curl around the fringes of your consciousness, wisps of meaning you see or hear or feel. And when they occur, jot them down on paper for later reflection.

One way we can learn the value of such insights is by comparing them to the understanding and experience of others. In matters of faith, it is helpful and wise to compare our own insights with those found in scripture, in the teaching of the church, and in the writings of religious scholars.

Good-Habit Builder

Each day for the next week, choose an appropriate time and place for cultivating silence and opening your mind and heart to God. Try to extend your time each day so

that by the end of the week you spend fifteen minutes.
Keep a daily record of the thoughts that occur to you.

Set Spiritual Goals

These days almost everyone has physical or athletic
goals. We want to lighten our weight by ten or twenty
pounds, firm up our bellies, reduce our waists, transform
flab into muscle. Or we want to improve our backhand
in tennis or eliminate the slice in our golf game. We also
have intellectual and emotional goals, such as thinking
before acting and exercising greater control over our
feelings.

When it comes to spiritual matters, however, many of
us have only a vague notion of our goals: "being a better
person," for example, or "getting closer to God." But
vague goals are not likely to be achieved, so if we want
to grow spiritually, we must be as diligent about setting
spiritual goals as we are about physical and intellectual
ones.

What are spiritual goals and how do they differ from
other goals? In many cases spiritual goals are inter-
twined with and almost indistinguishable from intellectual and moral goals. But an important difference is in
the motivation behind them. Whenever our main purpose is to make ourselves more pleasing to God, the goal
may be considered spiritual. In other words, if we decide to expand our knowledge of geography or history
or language because doing so will help us in our job or
make us a better conversationalist, our goal (though
worthwhile) would not be spiritual. But if our purpose in
knowing is to develop our intellectual capability to show
God our appreciation for that gift, the goal is spiritual.

Making our lives reflect the Ten Commandments more
fully is a spiritual goal, as is becoming poor in spirit,
gentle, and merciful.

In setting your spiritual goals, take care not to frame

them only in the negative. There's nothing wrong with deciding, "I won't disobey my parents," "I won't take the Lord's name in vain," "I won't be selfish," and so on. But realize that they just say what you *won't* do. Force yourself to give expression to what you *will* do, and be as specific as you can. For example, say, "I'll make my thoughts, words, and actions demonstrate respect for my parents," "I'll speak the Lord's name often and always with reverence and love," and "I'll go out of my way to put others before myself."

Good-Habit Builder

Look at the contents page of this book. Review the specific habits listed there and ask which ones represent the most meaningful expression of your love for God. Make the development of those habits your spiritual goal. (The fact that you may have another motivation for developing them will in no way lessen their spiritual significance.) Place reminders of them where you will see them often.

Count Your Blessings

There's nothing necessarily wrong with wanting what we don't have, as long as the wanting is balanced with appreciation of what we do have. This age of commercialism, however, parades before us an endless array of material things and stimulates us to want in excess. As a result, we expect more than we have a right to, and when we don't get it, we can deceive ourselves into thinking that God has somehow deprived us of what is our due. It is one of the great ironies of our time that North Americans, who are among the most blessed human beings in history, are often unsatisfied and unappreciative.

The antidote to this spiritual condition is to develop

the habit of counting our blessings—that is, of reviewing frequently all that we have to be thankful for and
offering a prayer of thanksgiving. Because it asks for
nothing but expresses appreciation for everything, such
a prayer is especially pleasing to God.

Acknowledging that you are blessed can be difficult if
you have grown accustomed to comparing yourself with
people who have more than you. But you can easily
overcome that difficulty by imagining God has revealed
that you will die next week. (Since many people will die
between now and then, and it is entirely possible that
you could be one of them, the idea is not as farfetched as
it may seem.)

With this thought in mind, ask yourself what you want
to do with your final week. What sights and sounds and
tastes and experiences would be most important to you?
With what people would you spend that week? If you
were to list them all, there might be some new experiences: a visit to a city you'd never seen before, such as
Rome or Paris, or some exotic food you'd never tasted,
or meeting some celebrity. But chances are you'd want
to see and hear and taste and experience familiar things.

Suddenly all the things you normally take for granted
would be terribly important to you. You'd want to look at
your spouse's face and the faces of your children and
memorize every detail. You'd want to see every sunrise
and sunset, smell every flower, walk in the rain and let its
wetness caress you. Even the smallest things would evoke
a powerful emotional response: your dog, your tennis
racquet, photos of happy times, books, your old raincoat.

Let your mind range over all the hundreds of things
that are special to you and then realize that, quite probably, you are not going to die next week and all those
wonderful things and people you couldn't bear to leave
are still here to enrich your life. And then thank God for
them and for the breath and consciousness to enjoy
those blessings.

Finally, refuse to let this feeling of gratitude slip away. Keep it alive, renew it daily, and you will grow ever closer to God.

Good-Habit Builder

Make a list of the blessings God has provided for you. Include talents, relationships, answered prayers, treasured experiences, and occasions of grace. Keep this list nearby and reread it whenever you are tempted to feel sorry for yourself.

Recall Moments of Closeness to God

From time to time, usually around holidays, a magazine will run a special article on religious faith and ask a variety of people their experience of God. The responses range from passionate testimonies of faith all the way to equally passionate professions of agnosticism and atheism. Many people speak of times in their lives when they had an overpowering sense of God's presence. For some the experience is constant, for others recurrent, but there are always a number who never have the experience again. Though they wait for it and hope for it, it never returns. Always they are sad, and sometimes bitter.

Does God reveal himself only to certain people at times and places of his choosing? Or is God always here, desiring to be known by every human being but waiting for some initiative from us? Must we seek in order to find God? Does, perhaps, our wanting too much and trying too hard doom our efforts to experience God as surely as not wanting or trying? The answers to these questions may lie beyond human understanding.

One thing is certain, however. If we are fortunate enough to have felt God's presence, we do better to keep that memory alive, return to it, and be nourished by it than to worry about whether and when the experience will recur.

Was there such a special moment in your life? (Was there more than one?) When did it occur? What were the circumstances? Were you alone or with others? How old were you? Were you celebrating a special occasion, such as your confirmation or marriage? Recall where you were, what you were doing at the time. What was your state of mind? What were you thinking and feeling? Were you happy or sad? What was the experience like? Try to recall it now. Did you see something, a brightness perhaps? Did you actually see God or hear God's voice, or did you rather have a different physical sensation? How did the experience affect you then? Did it fill you with certainty, deepen your faith, move you to dedicate yourself to God? How does recalling it affect you now?

Your experience may be neither recurring nor dramatic. It may have occurred many years ago, in childhood, and have produced no more than a feeling of assurance that God created you and continues to care for you. However modest it may have been, remembering it will bring you closer to God.

Good-Habit Builder

Recall one special moment when you experienced God's presence. Review all the details of that moment to make the memory as vivid as possible. Try to feel now as you did then.

Confess Your Sins to God

Do you remember "The Rime of the Ancient Mariner," that famous poem by Samuel Taylor Coleridge? Generations of schoolchildren were required to memorize passages from it, like "Water, water, everywhere,/

And all the boards did shrink;/ Water, water, every-where,/ Nor any drop to drink," and "Alone, alone, all, all alone,/ Alone on a wide, wide sea!/ And never a saint took pity on/ My soul in agony." In case you are unfamil-iar with the poem, it tells the story of a man who was punished for the sin of killing an albatross. Part of his punishment was to carry the giant bird around his neck.

The poet's perspective may be unnecessarily dark, but the symbolism is apt. Many do carry the burden of their sins with them throughout their lives, but only because ignorance or pride prevents them from releasing them-selves. Others carry that burden to psychiatrists' couches in hopes of talking it away. They want to make the psychiatrist understand and to deepen their own un-derstanding. But what they really need, and what no hu-man can give, is God's forgiveness. The simple way to unburden ourselves of sin is to confess it to God. The way we do so is also important.

"Two men went up into the temple to pray, one a Pharisee, and the other a tax-gatherer. The Pharisee stood and was praying thus to himself, 'God, I thank Thee that I am not like other people: swindlers, unjust, adulterers, or even like this tax-gatherer. I fast twice a week; I pay tithes of all that I get.'

"But the tax-gatherer, standing some distance away, was even unwilling to lift up his eyes to heaven, but was beating his breast, saying, 'God, be merciful to me, the sinner!'

"I tell you [Jesus teaches], this man went down to his house justified rather than the other; for everyone who exalts himself shall be humbled, but he who humbles himself shall be exalted" (Luke 18:10–14).

The way to confess your sins before God is without qualifications, without excuses. If extenuating circum-stances lessen your guilt, God knows; you don't have to point it out. Doing so only dilutes your contrition. To

keep your shame in proper perspective, confess on your
knees. And have the right motive—don't confess merely
because you are afraid of punishment or want to relieve
yourself of the burden of your sins, but out of genuine
sorrow. Focus on the fact that God is goodness and love
and you chose to place some momentary, transitory
pleasure above obedience. Finally, incorporate into
your confession the desire to amend your life.

Good-Habit Builder

Confess your sins to God today. Then put a reminder in
your calendar to confess on a regular basis, perhaps once
a week or at least once a month.

Forgive Others' Offenses

In 1937 Gertrude Jamison's dog jumped over a hedge
and nipped newspaperboy A. Douglas Thompson on the
heel. He called the Humane Society and reported the
attack. For the next forty-five years Gertrude Jamison
nurtured her anger. She made his life miserable by calling Thompson as many as fifteen times a day and pester-
ing him. Even after she was jailed for harassment and
had a court-ordered padlock placed on her phone, she
found ways to continue. In 1982, at age eighty-four, she
was still at it.[7]

How many thousands of moments of bitterness and
negative emotions she could have spared herself by just
saying at the very moment it happened, or at least a day
later, "He did what he thought was right. I feel injured,
but I forgive him."

Few people behave as pathetically as did that disturbed woman. But many cause themselves and others
unnecessary pain by refusing to forgive, in some cases
even after the offender has apologized. There are people
who break off relations forever over some tiny, unin-

tended slight. (Indeed, in some cases the slight is only imagined.)

Yet others manage to forgive grave offenses. A woman I know learned that her husband and her best friend had had an ongoing affair for many years. She forgave them both and could even bring herself to offer condolences sometime later, when tragedy befell the friend. Another friend was bilked by her husband of all her savings, over $11,000. Still, she forgave him. Other people forgive their parents for neglecting, physically abusing, and even molesting them.

Forgiving others is not just a generous gesture. It is a requirement for fellowship with God. In Matthew 5:21–24 (JB), Jesus warns:

> You have learned how it was said to our ancestors: *You must not kill;* and if anyone does kill he must answer for it before the court. But I say this to you: anyone who is angry with his brother will answer for it before the court; if a man calls his brother "Fool" he will answer for it before the Sanhedrin; and if a man calls him "Renegade" he will answer for it in hell fire. So then, if you are bringing your offering to the altar and there remember that your brother has something against you, leave your offering there before the altar, go and be reconciled with your brother first, and then come back and present your offering.

It is significant that Jesus didn't say "anyone who was offended by his brother," but "anyone who is *angry* with his brother." His phrasing suggests it is unimportant which party, if either, was at fault. In other words, if someone offended you and you are angry, reconciliation is not just that person's obligation. It is yours too.

It may not be easy to forgive the other person. You may believe he or she doesn't *deserve* to be forgiven. You may feel justified in bearing your grudge. If that is the case, don't forgive for the other person's sake but out of love for God. And do it unconditionally.

Good-Habit Builder

Think of someone who offended you, either recently or a long time ago. Don't let the sun set on your anger another time. Reflect on Matthew 5:21–24 and let your anger go.

Renew a Broken Relationship

"Never hesitate to hold out your hand," wrote Pope John XXIII, "[and] never hesitate to accept the out-stretched hand of another." Wonderful spiritual advice, but it depends on someone taking the initiative. Unless you have a compelling reason not to be conciliatory, let that someone be you. (One good reason to avoid contact would be if the person had assaulted you.)

Once you have forgiven the other person in your heart, send a brief note saying you feel sad that your relationship was severed. Add that you'll call sometime soon and see if you can get together for dinner, a movie, or some other activity of mutual interest. After allowing sufficient time for the person to think about your letter, call and issue the invitation.

Expect your meeting to be somewhat awkward and strained. Should you talk about the incident that severed your relationship? That's a judgment you'll have to make at the time. Discussing it could reopen old wounds. (Consider, for example, how you'd react if told that the fault was entirely yours.) If the matter comes up, you might consider saying, "Our dispute denied us each other's companionship for the past month (year, decade). Let's not make the same mistake again."

Keep in mind that one person can't effect a reconciliation alone. It takes two. Some people, unfortunately, are not willing. So if you try, earnestly and humbly, yet are rebuffed, your conscience will be clear and you'll have the satisfaction of knowing you did the right thing.

Good-Habit Builder

Think of a broken relationship that you would like to repair. Make it a relationship which you were at least partly responsible for breaking. Write to the other person today, extending the hand of reconciliation. After an appropriate interval, call the person.

Nourish Your Soul with Good Reading

The belief that no one was ever hurt by a book is fashionable today. It is precisely this notion that underlies today's tolerance of material that would be considered obscene or blasphemous by our grandparents. And some of the people who believe that books can't do harm are the very same ones who stress the value of literature, especially the classics. It can't be both ways. Either books have power or they don't. If good books can ennoble and inspire us, bad books can corrupt us. (It does not necessarily follow, however, that bad books should be censored. This issue doesn't concern us here.)

The meaning of "good reading" depends on context. In a business context, good reading is that which helps us become more knowledgeable and sensitive about business. In the context of citizenship, it is reading that broadens our understanding of candidates and issues. In the context of spiritual growth, it is that which turns our thoughts toward God, deepens our understanding of religious truths, and encourages us to develop and maintain the habits associated with spirituality.

The simple formula "Only the Bible and books about the Bible may be classed as spiritual reading" is *overly* simple. In other words, it is mistaken. If we bring a religious sensibility to the task, a history or anthropology or psychology book or even a good novel can turn our thoughts to God.

How can you tell, before you buy or borrow a book or

magazine, whether it is likely to be spiritually nourishing? By glancing at the contents. A magazine's cover or contents page will often include brief summaries of the information within. Read these or skim the stories themselves. Similarly, a book's dust jacket and preface will usually provide a good indication of the author's message. If you are still uncertain, select a representative chapter from the contents and skim it.

You may wish to have your name put on the mailing list of a comprehensive religious book distributor. Your pastor will undoubtedly be able to recommend one to you.

Good-Habit Builder

Visit a religious bookstore, or the religion section of a secular bookstore, or your library. Browse through the offerings and select one or more titles that speak to spiritual questions important in your life. Purchase them or, in the case of the library, borrow them. (When you visit your library, ask the librarian to help you find a listing and description of current magazines specializing in spiritual matters.)

See God in Other People

Legend has it that Francis of Assisi, while walking across a plain, saw a figure approaching in the distance. As the figure came closer, Francis realized the man was a leper. In thirteenth-century Europe nothing was more frightening or loathsome than leprosy, for which there was no known cure. (Lepers were required to carry bells and shout "Unclean!" so that passersby could avoid them.) So Francis was tempted to shun the man. Yet he knew that the real test of faith is not how well we treat people of wealth, power, and influence but how well we treat the weak, the poor, the wretched.

As the leper drew nearer, Francis saw that the disease had ravaged the man's face. The ugliness and the stench repelled him, but he approached the leper, embraced him and kissed the rotting flesh of his cheek, then walked away. After proceeding only a few steps, Francis turned and saw nothing. Though the plain stretched out, flat and broad, in every direction, the leper had vanished.

Did the incident actually happen or was it created by a pious Franciscan biographer? If it did happen, was the leper a projection of Francis' imagination or did Christ actually appear to him to test his love? We have no way of knowing. But we do know that the lesson in the story is as valid today as it was seven hundred years ago: The way to fulfill Christ's command to love our neighbor is to look beneath outward appearances and look for a reflection of God's goodness and love.

It is not always easy to find that reflection. In many cases it is hidden beneath layers of ugliness—not so much the ugliness of physical disease, like that of the leper, but the ugliness of moral and spiritual disease. The bad habits, personal failings, and sins of others may prompt us to doubt that any sign of God's love is present; and doubt will blind us to that love.

Doubt has other causes than people's flaws: our own pride, for example. Pride can lead us to deny the power of the Holy Spirit to inhabit those who do not believe in God, or those who believe but do not share our particular theology. Thus many Christians never think of looking for God in an atheist or an agnostic, a Hindu or a Muslim, a Jew or a Mormon. They assume God has nothing to do with such people. (Not infrequently, Catholics and Protestants make the same assumption about each other.)

God created all people, not just those who share our beliefs. And he gave every person gifts of mind and heart. Even the tiniest of human virtues—a feeling for the underdog, tenderness toward children, reluctance to injure others, appreciation of beauty—are reflections of God's goodness. The Holy Spirit can work quietly in people, enlarging these virtues, investing the natural with the supernatural. Seek these little qualities in other people you meet, and you will find God in them and find a reason for loving them.

But what of the case of outspoken atheists, who loudly proclaim their hatred of God and contempt for all religion? Is it possible that the Holy Spirit is present in them? As long as it is possible for the human heart to be converted, the answer is yes. Remember that rejection of God, and even blasphemy, may reach its zenith just before conversion.

Good-Habit Builder

Practice looking for God in everyone you meet today. Start with a person who, from outward appearances, seems a most unlikely candidate.

Open Your Heart to Everyday Grace

Grace, in the formal sense, means the freely given and unmerited favor and love of God. It is usually associated with the sacraments of the church, but there is another kind of grace as well. It might be called everyday grace, because it is not confined to special religious occasions or rituals but is always and everywhere available.

Everyday grace is the inspiration and insight contained in the events of our lives. God communicates to us through our experiences, filling them with meaning, with lessons that can deepen our understanding and lead us to wisdom. But it is up to us to extract that meaning and use it to guide our lives.

To open your heart to everyday grace, begin each day with this prayer:

Heavenly Father, I know you will speak to me many times today in what I see and hear. Help me grasp the meaning of each experience and apply it to my spiritual benefit.

As the day's events unfold, consider how they speak to you. Seeing a funeral procession may remind you of the brevity of life and urge you to put your spiritual affairs in order. Observing an elderly woman limping along with a cane may turn your thoughts to your parents and their need to be included in your life. Noticing a mother shouting at her child in public may chastise you for your own impatience as a parent.

A single event can carry several messages. A seeing eye dog leading its master may speak to you of faithful devotion or of the blessings of sight or of the need for strength in adversity. The unabashed joy of people as they greet one another at an airport may remind you that the love of family is more precious than gold.

Good-Habit Builder

Begin tomorrow with the above prayer and keep your heart open to everyday grace throughout the day.

Translate Your Faith Into Action

The Word is a singularly important symbol for Christians because it refers to Jesus: "In the beginning was the Word, and the Word was with God, and *the Word was God*. . . . And the Word became flesh, and dwelt among us, and we beheld His glory, glory as of the only begotten from the Father, full of grace and truth" (John 1:1–14). Its importance is further reflected in many other references. The Bible speaks of the word of God, the word of truth, the word of life, servants of the Word, and the word of faith.

If we are not careful, however, this emphasis on the word (and Word), together with the many biblical references to proclaiming our faith and exhortations to pray, can narrow our perspective—that is, can make us content with verbal expressions. But saying is not enough; it must be matched by doing.

Jesus advises us, "Let your light shine before men in such a way that they may see your good works, and glorify your Father who is in heaven" (Matt. 5:16). And again, "You will know them by their fruits. Grapes are not gathered from thorn bushes, nor figs from thistles, are they? . . . Not everyone who says to me, 'Lord, Lord,' will enter the kingdom of heaven; but he who does the will of my Father who is in heaven" (Matt. 7:16, 21).

And James explains, "What use is it, my brethren, if a man says he has faith, but he has no works? Can that faith save him? If a brother or sister is without clothing and in need of daily food, and one of you says to them, 'Go in peace, be warmed and be filled,' and yet you do not give them what is necessary for their body, what use is that? . . . Just as the body without the spirit is dead, so also faith without works is dead" (James 2:14–16, 26).

Be sure that your spirituality is a matter of deeds as well as of words. To maintain the right balance between the two, keep in mind this wise old saying: "Pray as if everything depended on God; work as if everything depended on you."

Good-Habit Builder

Think of as many ways as you can to translate your faith into action. Decide what you can do to meet people's physical, financial, emotional, intellectual, and spiritual needs. Then act on your decision.

Epilogue

A journey of a thousand miles, says the ancient Chinese proverb, begins with a single step. It is the same with forming a good habit. A single action begins the process, and frequent repetition achieves your goal. By completing the good-habit builders in this book you have taken many first steps toward self-improvement. Now your challenge is to repeat each of them, making it a part of your daily routine of thinking, feeling, and doing.

Meeting this challenge will not be easy. When novelty fades, distractions will multiply, fatigue will set in, and you will be tempted to quit. Moreover, popular culture, with its incessant message of impulsiveness, instant gratification, and self-indulgence, will undermine your efforts and threaten your resolve. To overcome these obstacles, you will have to remind yourself often that the popular view of life is empty and that genuine self-improvement demands continuing effort and self-discipline.

Some will try to persuade you that psychology opposes this demanding view of life and self-improvement. In fact, some psychologists do counsel accepting yourself as you are rather than becoming something better. But others argue that mental health is achieved by *transcending* the self. Viktor Frankl is one of these. We discussed him in chapter 9, noting that he used his experiences in a Nazi concentration camp to probe the human mind and heart and found that the drive to make sense out of our lives is more fundamental in human beings than the sex drive and the drive for power.

How did Frankl and other inmates of the camps overcome the sense of futility and utter despair that was an inevitable result of their experience? "We had to learn," he explains,

> that it did not really matter what we expected from life, but rather what life expected from us. We needed to stop asking about the meaning of life, and instead to think of ourselves as those who were being questioned by life— daily and hourly. Our answer must consist, not in talk and meditation, but in right action and in right conduct.[8]

Unlike psychologists who advise removing all tension from our lives, Frankl argues that the tension of finding and living values is essential. Mental health, he argues,

> is based on a certain degree of tension, the tension between what one has already achieved and what one still ought to accomplish, or the gap between what one is and what one should become. Such a tension is inherent in the human being and therefore is indispensable to mental well-being. . . . What man actually needs is not a tensionless state but rather the striving and struggling for some goal worthy of him. What he needs is not the discharge of tension at any cost, but the call of a potential meaning waiting to be fulfilled by him.[9]

Each of us, in Frankl's view, "is questioned by life; and he can only answer to life by *answering for* his own life; to life he can only respond by being responsible." And he disagrees with those who claim that neurotics need a less demanding way. He believes that some neurosis is caused by the failure to find meaning and a sense of responsibility. And, he reasons, "If architects want to strengthen a decrepit arch, they *increase* the load that is laid upon it, for thereby the parts are joined more firmly together."[10]

The struggle to become more than we are and all that we can be is the central challenge of being human. Though we have a special dignity because we are created in the image and likeness of God, the fullness of our humanity is not given; it must be earned. No use of our minds is more fundamental than understanding this fact and working out its implications in our lives. No use of our wills is more important than to commit ourselves to acting on this knowledge.

To gain the necessary strength to continue developing good habits, dedicate your efforts to God. Regard every good-habit builder you practice as a prayer. Let it express, in a way more meaningful than words alone, your appreciation and your love. And let it be your humble response to the question that captives of popular culture cannot answer: "What am I doing to make my life count for something larger than self?"

Here is a final good-habit builder, one designed to ensure that the others will thrive.

Good-Habit Builder

Keep this book handy and mark your calendar to review it at the beginning of every month. At those times, decide which habits need further nurturing. Then renew your effort.

Notes

1. Robert H. Schuller, *Self-Esteem: The New Reformation* (Waco, Tex.: Word Books, 1982), 14, 19, 33, 67, 98.

2. Nancy Larrick, "Children of Television," *Teacher*, September 1975, 75-77.

3. David L. Rosenhan, "On Being Sane in Insane Places," *Science*, 1983, 179:250-258.

4. One of the best sources of past and current research on creativity is the Creative Studies Institute at the University of Buffalo (New York). The institute publishes the *Journal of Creative Behavior*.

5. Tom Mathews, "Fine Art or Foul?" *Newsweek*, July 2, 1990, 46-52.

6. Jerre Levy, "Research Synthesis on Right and Left Hemispheres," *Educational Leadership* 40, No. 4 (January 1983), 66-71.

7. Robert Fulghum, *All I Really Need to Know I Learned in Kindergarten* (New York: Villard Books, 1988), 19-20.

8. *New York Times*, October 17, 1982, 32.

9. Viktor E. Frankl, *Man's Search for Meaning* (New York: Washington Square Press, 1963), 122.

10. Ibid., 165-166.

11. Ibid., 172, 167.